EYES OF THE HUSKY

MW00721136

Skookum's Penetrating Insights into the Hearts & Minds of Northerners

EYES OF THE HUSKY

Skookum's Penetrating Insights into the Hearts & Minds of Northerners

by Doug Urquhart

Lost Moose Publishing, Whitehorse, Yukon

Copyright © 2000 by Doug Urquhart

All rights reserved. No part of this book may be reproduced or transmitted in any form, by any means, without written permission from the publisher, except by a reviewer, who may quote brief passages in a review. The author encourages non-commercial copying of his work for slide shows, newsletters, and other media which are intended to shed light on northern life. However, permission must first be sought directly from the author by sending a fax of the strip you intend to use with a note about where and when it is to be used. (Fax 867-668-5622)

Published by:
Lost Moose Publishing
58 Kluane Crescent
Whitehorse, Yukon Y1A 3G7 Canada
phone (867) 668-5076, fax (867) 668-6223
lmoose@yknet.yk.ca
www.yukonweb.com/business/lost_moose

Canadian Cataloguing in Publication Data

Urquhart, Doug
Eyes of the Husky : Skookum's penetrating insights into the hearts and minds of northerners

ISBN 1-896758-05-3

1. Comic books, strips, etc., Canadian (English)
2. Canada, Northern -- Social conditions -- Comic books, strips, etc.
3. Skookum (Fictitious character)

PN6734.U76 2000 741.5'971 C00-980257-6

Printed and bound in Canada.

Contents

WHAT THE HECK ARE YOU DOING?!
'PAWS' IS 16 YEARS OLD! YOU SHOULD TELL FOLKS HOW IT WAS CREATED!

C'MON! EVERY ARTIST WANTS TO TALK ABOUT HIS WORK!
WELL... OKAY!

I REMEMBER IT WAS A JANUARY NIGHT 19 YEARS AGO IN YELLOWKNIFE WHEN I SAT DOWN TO DRAW THE FIRST STRIP...

AS AN EXPERIENCED CARTOONIST, I FIGURED THIS SHOULD BE PRETTY EASY...

BUT AFTER A COUPLE OF HOURS I REALIZED I DIDN'T HAVE A CLUE ABOUT CARTOON STRIPS!!

There was so little space

My speech bubbles had way too many words so that I had no room left over to draw any characters at all!

I didn't know how to draw the same person
from different angles

AND MY STORIES WERE TOO LONG FOR A SINGLE STRIP!!!

EVENTUALLY I LEARNED TO...

OPEN MY SPEECH BUBBLES, COMPRESS TEXT AND CUT BODIES TO GAIN SPACE!!

DRAW BORDERS FREEHAND FOR SPEED AND INTEREST!
AND AVOID MESSY INK AND RULERS!

AND VARY ANGLES AND PERSPECTIVES, LIKE MOVIE SHOTS!

AND USE OPEN BOXES IF I RAN OUT OF ROOM!!

THEN I HAD TO CREATE CHARACTERS...

SKOOKUM:
SINCE THE STRIP WAS ABOUT THE NORTH, I THOUGHT A DOG TEAM WOULD BE BEST WITH THE LEADER AS HERO. IT TOOK ME 2 YEARS AFTER THE STRIP BEGAN TO FIND THE PERFECT NAME.

'SKOOKUM' IS ORIGINALLY FROM THE CHILCOTIN TRADING LANGUAGE AND IS COMMONLY USED IN THE NORTH TO MEAN CLEVER, IMAGINATIVE, STURDY. SKOOKUM JIM DISCOVERED GOLD IN THE KLONDIKE IN 1896.

- TWISTED EARS FOR VERSATILITY IN EXPRESSION AND BECAUSE SNEAKY DOGS ARE ALWAYS LISTENING IN ALL DIRECTIONS
- EXAGGERATED HUSKY/WOLF FACE WHICH EVEN IN REAL LIFE HAVE MARKINGS TO DRAMATIZE EXPRESSIONS
- COMPRESSED BODY AND HUGE HUSKY FEET – WHENCE THE NAME 'PAWS'

SKOOKUM'S TEAM

RUFUS:
FEATURES ALL OPPOSITE TO SKOOKUM

PSYCHO:
COLOUR OPPOSITE TO SKOOKUM

FUBSY:

STYLED OPPOSITE TO OTHERS. A TYPICAL HAPPY-GO-LUCKY WHEEL DOG.

MARTEN:

- SHARP FEATURES
- HUNCHED SHOULDERS
- MACKINAW COAT
- STYLIZED LEGS AND FEET TO MATCH DOGS AND FOCUS ATTENTION ON UPPER BODY.

SKOOKUM'S OBVIOUS PARTNER IS A TRAPPER WHO I NAMED **'MARTEN FISHER'** AFTER TWO NORTHERN FURBEARERS. HE HAS SHARP FEATURES AND DARK HAIR TO REPRESENT A TYPICAL NORTHERNER WITH SOME FIRST NATION ANCESTRY.

SUPPORTING CAST...

THE PAL

VICTOR CONIBEAR (NAMED AFTER TWO TRAP MANUFACTURERS) IS A TOTAL CONTRAST TO MARTEN, BEING ROUND AND STOCKY WHERE MARTEN IS SHARP FEATURED AND THIN.

THE WIVES

ROSIE AND PHOEBE ARE COUSINS AND ARE DRAWN IDENTICALLY EXCEPT FOR THE HAIR

THE KIDS

'WINCH'- SHORT FOR WINCHESTER IS ROSIE AND MARTEN'S SON. HIS FEMININE COUNTERPART IS A COUSIN.

THE SOUTHERN FRIENDS

HAL (NAMED AFTER THE 2001 SPACE ODYSSEY COMPUTER) IS A COMPUTER SALESMAN WITH A STRANGE ATTRACTION TO THE NORTH. HE AND HIS WIFE, GWEN, ARE STRAIGHT MEN FOR SOUTHERN JOKES.

DYNAMICS & CONTENT...

I WAS SUPRISED TO LEARN THAT SOLVING STRIP MECHANICS AND CREATING CHARACTERS WAS NOT THE END BUT ONLY LEAD TO MORE DECISIONS!! WOULD SKOOKUM TALK DIRECTLY TO MARTEN (NO OTHER STRIP DOES THIS)? WOULD MARTEN TALK TO OTHER ANIMALS?

ONCE I TOOK THE FIRST STEP OF SKOOKUM SPEAKING TO MARTEN, THE REST EVOLVED SO THAT MARTEN CONVERSES WITH EVERYTHING INCLUDING ROCKS AND TREES WHICH IS TRULY HOW YOU FEEL WHEN YOU LIVE IN THE BUSH!

HI!
HI!
HI!
HI!
HI!

AND A FURTHER STEP IS THAT I CAN ALSO TALK DIRECTLY TO YOU! THIS LET'S ME DESCRIBE SITUATIONS AND MAKE WITTY ASIDES!!

AND FINALLY THERE'S

IDEAS !!!

THIS IS WHERE MANY GOOD ARTISTS BOG DOWN! I KEEP A NOTE BOOK

IN MY HIP POCKET TO WRITE DOWN IDEAS FROM...

MEETINGS

THE BAR

TOURISTS

FAMILY

VISITORS

SHOPS

PILOTS

ELDERS

...AND THE BUSH !!

THEMES...

NOT SUPRISINGLY, WHEN INTENSE CHARACTERS ARE PUT IN A RICH ENVIRONMENT, THEY TEND TO TAKE OVER AND FROM THIS DYNAMIC (MY OBSERVATIONS AND THEIR RESPONSES) SEVERAL MAIN THEMES HAVE EMERGED THAT PORTRAY THE ESSENCE OF THE NORTHERNER AND THEIR LIVES AND TIMES.

The Bush

1994

Love of the land and freedom to be in it are the paramount joys for northerners from which all else flows. Life in the bush is like entering another world where perceptions are vastly altered and realities become highly subjective. Unfortunately, all this is very hard to communicate to others and thus northerners often appear less intelligent and thoughtful than they really are, confirming southern impressions that northerners are simply ignorant rustics.

THREE MONTHS ALONE IN THE BUSH...
OH...OH.
© D. URQUHART

WE'RE A RICH COUNTRY TO OWN ALL THIS LAND RIGHT?!!
NOBODY OWNS IT! WE'RE JUST HERE TO LOOK AFTER IT AND PASS IT ON TO GOOD HANDS!
00-04

YOUR TRAPPER FRIEND DOESN'T EXPRESS HIMSELF VERY WELL
MAYBE, BUT HE'S A GENIUS IN THE BUSH! HUNTING, TRAPPING, GUIDING FISHING, PROSPECTING LOGGING, ANYTHING HE CAN DO!!
© D. URQUHART

YEEOWW!

OH! DID YOU GET A BIG BOOBOO ON YOUR PATTY PAW?
AND WOULD YOU WIKE A HUG AND A BIG BANDAGE?
YESH! (SNIFF!)
YESH! (SIGH!)

AH NUTHIN' REALLY! BUT ROSIE SURE FREAKED OUT!!
94-7

The macho image is as vital to the northern self image as the ball cap and mackinaw jacket. But as this strip demonstrates, every macho northerner is still a multiple personality. The dark smokey bar scenery I picked up from another cartoonist.

FIRST YOU LET AN OLD FRIDGE AND STOVE RUST IN YOUR YARD FOR 6 OR 7 YEARS...
94-2

MEANWHILE YOU GET PAILS, WOOD AND OTHER STUFF YOU'LL NEED...
© D. URQUHART

THEN PUT THE STOVE RACKS IN THE FRIDGE AND FIRE HER UP!!
SMOKING FISH IS SO TECHNICAL!

HEY! I'M A PROFESSIONAL!

A friend of mine in Atlin built a smoker just this way. Virtually every Atlin home has a stash of metal and wood junk somewhere on the property which is essential for all kinds of low cost constructions and repairs. My patch featured all kinds of bicycle parts salvaged from the dump.

QUITTING ALREADY? CAN'T HACK THE BUSH LIFE, EH?
IT'S NOT THAT! BUT MARTEN'S SINGING IS DRIVING ME NUTS!
94-4
OH MY NAME IS JON JOHNSEN! I COME FROM VISCONSIN...
TRY THESE!
ISE DA BYE DAT BUILDS DEE BOAT
KIDS TODAY CAN'T HACK THE BUSH WITHOUT SOME ELECTRONIC CRUTCH!
© D.URQUHART

There is a constant tension in the north between those who value bush knowledge and skills and those (usually young people) who find bush life boring. I experience this on occasion with my teenagers and it is a vital concern for First Nations elders who wish to pass on their traditional knowledge to younger generations. Consequently, any teenager in the bush is scrutinized closely for signs of boredom or inattention and, as in this strip, misunderstandings can arise.

1994

UNT VEN ZEE ZALMON ALL GONE I SHOOT TWO COW MOOSE FOR SUMMER EXPLORATIONS!
FREE LIFE! FREE LAND! by WOLFGANG BULLMEISTER
© D. URQUHART

UNT ZEN I AVE KILL ONE GRIZZLY FOR SAFETY UNT ZIX CARIBOU FOR CLOTHINGS UNT ZEN...

UNT ZEN TO JAIL FOR BREAKING ZIX BIG GAME LAWS!!
94-5

A friend told me about a slide show he had seen in Germany featuring a European adventurer who portrayed the north just like this. Every several years there is a newspaper story about some European who has been "caught" living off the land.

ALL DAY LONG WITHOUT A BREAK! I CAN'T TAKE IT!!

MARTEN BROKE HIS PROMISE SO HE DESERVES THIS!
RIP!
CRUNCH!
CRACK!
© D. URQUHART
94-6
DOES THE WORD CLAUSTROPHOBIA MEAN ANYTHING TO YOU?!!

On the long dog-racing circuit you often see doors chewed out by bored, cramped huskies.

NORTHERNERS NEED... ..(NOPE!).. NORTHERNERS DEMAND.. A... A GREATER
© D. URQUHART

..SAY..(NOPE) INPUT TO WILDLIFE AFFAIRS..(NO) MANAGEMENT ISSUES...

WELL HECK! 5 DAYS ON THE TRAPLINE..
94-7
BUT MY BRAIN NEVER LEFT TOWN!!!

I go through this every time I walk in the bush. I have to stop and mentally focus on my surroundings or otherwise I can complete the entire walk totally immersed in the minutia of petty life.

SO THAT'S ... UH ... HOW WE ... UH FEEL ... THANKS!!

YOUR TRAPPER FRIEND DOESN'T EXPRESS HIMSELF VERY WELL
MAYBE, BUT HE'S A GENIUS IN THE BUSH! HUNTING, TRAPPING, GUIDING FISHING, PROSPECTING LOGGING, ANYTHING HE CAN DO!!
© D. URQUHART

SO?!!
94-8

Working for more than a decade for the Porcupine Caribou Management Board, I have seen this happen on many occasions. However, northerners, and particularly First Nations people, can also hold a southern audience spellbound when they just relax and tell their story.

IT WAS JUST ANOTHER KUNG-FU MOVIE IN THE GREAT WHITE NORTH!
© D. URQUHART
94-9

DRIVING DOGS BACK AND FORTH WITH THE DIRECTOR SHOUTING MO' FASTAH, MO' SLOWAH WHAT A DRAG!!
OH! MR. MARTEN YOO-HOO!!

MR. MARTEN YOU ARE SO BRAVE AND FUNNY! THAT PARTY AFTER YOU SAVED LING AND THEN THE SAUNA! OOOOO!!

The north is a popular location for movies, TV dramas and commercials. I once saw the Grand Chief of the Council for Yukon First Nations posing as an Inuit hunter for a frozen bagel commercial. In a Kung-fu movie shot in Atlin, they hauled a giant plastic ice cube, with the heroine inside it, across a frozen lake. At the end of the shooting, the actors and crew hosted a legendary party at the Atlin Inn where the leading lady enchanted the locals with cabaret songs.

NOT LONG NOW AND WE'LL BE SAFE!!
BLAM!
BLAM!
BLAM!
© D. URQUHART
SEE!
GAME SANCTUARY
AND YOU DIDN'T BELIEVE IN FORCE-FIELDS!
94-10

This strip comes from hunting stories near the Kluane Game Sanctuary where it is legal to hunt on one side of the Alaska Highway but not the other. Thus, a hot pursuit may be suddenly terminated as the hunted animal runs across the road into the posted sanctuary.

AND SO NOW THE ANALYSIS INCORPORATES TRADITIONAL KNOWLEDGE
WOW! YOU GUYS ACTUALLY WENT TO THE ARCTIC TO TALK TO THE ELDERS?
NO, WE GOT A TRADITIONAL KNOWLEDGE PROGRAM FROM COMPUTER SYSTEMS INC.
IT SAYS NAVAJO ELDERS DESCRIBE PEYOTE RITUAL!
THERE'S A DIFFERENCE?
BUT IT'S SO COMPATIBLE WITH OUR SOFTWARE!!
94-11
©D.URQUHART

This came from a story told to me by my friend, Gary, who was a PhD anthropology student at the time. All over the world, city-raised bureaucrats are grappling with the concept of traditional knowledge. What they need is to spend serious time with elders on the land. What they want is a handy reference they can plug into their office systems.

THE PROBLEM DOMAIN IS THE FUNCTIONAL SOCIAL SYSTEM WHICH IS CONCEPTUALIZED BY PROCESSES THAT...

THE CONTEXTUAL INCENTIVES ORIENT TOWARDS A VISION BUILDING PROCESS WHICH MERGES WITH IDENTIFIABLE COLLABORATIVE PROCESSES THAT
© D. URQUHART

...UM.. THAT... UM I DON'T KNOW WHAT I'M SAYING!
I COULD THINK OF A WORD!
94-12

I juggled this from some writing by my graduate student friend, Gary. Later, by mistake, I read it to him over the phone. There was an embarrassed pause and then he said, "Doug, I wrote that!" We had a good laugh in the end.

WELL, THIS IS THE BEST AXE BUT THIS IS $2.95 CHEAPER SO, I'LL GET IT!

BECAUSE THAT'S HOW NORTHERNERS LIVE BELOW THE
© D. URQUHART
94-13

POVERTY LINE RIGHT?

FORTY-SIX? HERE'S A FIFTY CHARLENE KEEP THE CHANGE!!

A trapper and salmon fisherman from Dawson City was flipping through the draft of this book and at this strip said, "I'm just as guilty!" Me too.

I FULLY SUPPORT YOUR PROJECT AND WILL ARRANGE FOR FUNDING..
WOW! THE GOVERNOR'S SUPPORT! HOW DID WE GET THAT?!
BECAUSE I WROTE IT!
©D.URQUHART

SEE? I HELP YOU MAKE A GOOD PROPOSAL TO THE GOVERNMENT...
AND IT GETS SENT DOWN THE LINE UNTIL SOMEBODY CAN RESPOND TO IT INTELLIGENTLY!
SO I WIND UP ANSWERING MY OWN LETTER!

94-14
SO WHY DO WE ELECT ALL THOSE OTHER GUYS?!!

This actually happened when I was working as Executive Director of the Porcupine Caribou Management Board.

I NOTICED THE RABBITS ARE REALLY UP THIS SPRING!
YOU DID? WE SHOULD CHECK THAT WITH OUR MODEL!
©D.URQUHART

I CAN DOWNLOAD THE STATS BY MODEM TO YOUR MAINFRAME
I'LL WORK THE GRAPHICS ON WINDOWS FOR RABBITS!
I'LL PUT OUT A CALL FOR DATA ON WEB
I'LL DO A LITERATURE SEARCH ON ECO-NET
I'LL FORMAT YOUR WORK FOR PUBLICATION!
YOU'RE LUCKY TO OBSERVE REAL WILDERNESS SCIENCE IN ACTION!!
94-15

I attended a presentation about a 10-year arctic hare study at a research station in the Yukon. Someone asked if local knowledge had been incorporated into the project. The answer was, "We found we could not get locals to follow the research procedures properly."

WELL THIS APPLICANT IS DISQUALIFIED AS THE GOVERNMENT CHARTER PROHIBITS

ANYONE WITH A PRISON RECORD!
94-16
NEW TO THE NORTH AREN'T YOU?
©D.URQUHART

There were only two of us in Atlin who did local jail guarding and we joked that it was because we were the only ones who could pass the RCMP security test. It used to be in the north that you never asked a newcomer what he or she did in the past or where they came from or even their last name. The north was essentially a clean slate for misfits and I am sure many people have profited from the chance to escape their past and start afresh.

SAW RALPH TODAY WITH MIKE AND SARAH! LOOKS LIKE HIS FOOT IS OKAY NOW
GREAT! SARAH WAS REAL BORED WHILE HE WAS OUT OF COMMISSION
YEAH AND MIKE TOOK UP WITH JAKE AND WILLY
BAD MOVE! JAKE'S ALL TROUBLE AND WILLY JUST COPIES HIM!
Hi SARAH! MIKE MY MAN! FOOT LOOKS GOOD RALPH!
©D. URQUHART
I GOTTA GET OUT OF THIS TOWN!
94-17

In small towns you not only know everybody, you know all the local dogs as well. One giant husky named "Lobo" used to hang out at the tourist campground in Atlin. He wore a ridiculous red ribbon with a sign that said, "Don't feed me, I have a home!" If your dog was missing you could strategically phone around until you had its location pretty well pinpointed.

...THEN THERE'S THE ARCTIC SINK WHICH COLLECTS HEAVY METALS FROM THE SOUTH!
©D. URQUHART
NOT TO MENTION RADIO-NUCLEIDES TOXAPHENES AND ARCTIC HAZE!!
94-18
WHAT'S THAT?
AH, JUST THE TOWN EFFLUENT PIPE, NOW AS I WAS SAYING...

Northerners are quick to point out what science tells us about our vulnerability to southern pollution. Less quick are we to acknowledge our own flaws. The Whitehorse sewage issue raged for years. European tourists, questing for the pristine north, regularly paddled among floating turds on their way down the Yukon River to Lake LaBerge. Thanks to the Yukon Conservation Society, a full treatment system was eventually installed.

THEY COLLECT ENERGY FROM THE STARS...
©D. URQUHART
94-19
CHANNEL IT INTO THEIR HOMES...
...SO THEY CAN GET RECHARGED EVERY NIGHT!
AND YOU STILL DON'T BELIEVE THEY ARE ALIENS!!

The most incongruous sight in the north is a log cabin village flanked by satellite dishes as big as the houses themselves. To the science-fiction-minded it could be an outpost for extraterrestrials.

OH WINCHESTER! YOU'RE WEARING BILLY'S SWEATER!
© D. URQUHART

HE WAS SO ADORABLE IN IT **AND SO CUDDLY!**

94-20
WHEN I HAVE KIDS I WILL NEVER DRESS THEM FROM **THE LOCAL RUMMAGE!!!**

For many years we outfitted our entire family from the Anglican Church rummage in Atlin. Moms would often stop to remark about owning the same outfit when their kids were younger. One of Whitehorse's most important gatherings is the monthly rummage sale at "Mary House" where you get to fill a green garbage bag for $1.

SO WHAT DO YOU THINK OF THE NEW GROCERY STORE?
SOFT BREAD! GREAT BBQ CHICKEN!!

94-21
PACKAGES TEAR EASY!
YEP! AND PLASTIC CARTONS PUNCTURE GOOD!
©D. URQUHART

I THINK I'LL STOP BY THIS STORE AGAIN!
ME, TOO! SEE YUH!

Typical scene outside the grocery stores in Whitehorse, Yellowknife and Inuvik. This is a case where you have a simple idea – ravens raid groceries in truck boxes – but you need to make a "gag" out of it for an interesting cartoon.

94-22
YEP! ONLY $17,900 FOR THIS BABY AND IT GETS 38 MILES TO THE GALLON!
©D. URQUHART

HOW COME YOU STILL DRIVE THAT OLD GAS GUZZLER MARTEN?

WELL, MAINLY BECAUSE IT ONLY COST $600...
...WHICH GIVES ME $17,300 LEFT OVER **FOR GAS!!**

I have a friend who recently bought a new vehicle that costs more than all the ones I have ever owned. But it gets good mileage.

1994

LIVED HERE LONG?
94-23-
ALL MY LIFE!

SHOT A MOOSE RIGHT THERE WHEN I WAS 20!
©D.URQUHART

NOW THAT'S **AN OLDTIMER!**

I have met several old timers with stories like these. The latest one was in the bowels of Scarborough ("Scarberia") Ontario where a fellow told me about hunting pheasants in what is now a monster subdivision. Black silhouettes, as in panel 3, are useful to focus attention on small figures.

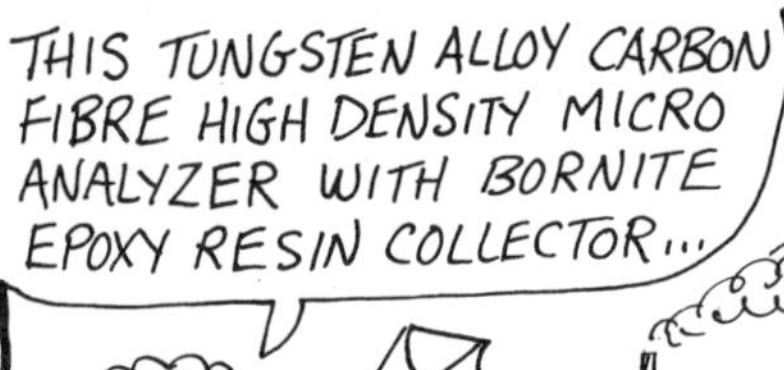
THIS TUNGSTEN ALLOY CARBON FIBRE HIGH DENSITY MICRO ANALYZER WITH BORNITE EPOXY RESIN COLLECTOR...

MAKES THIS THE LATEST IN INDUSTRIAL POLLUTION DETECTION TECHNOLOGY!
©D.URQUHART

AND THINK OF ALL THE INDUSTRIAL POLLUTION IT TOOK TO PRODUCE IT!!
94-24

We are techno junkies. We love to increase the sophistication of our knowledge at the expense of our environment to show us how rapidly we are destroying our environment through the sophistication of our society. The entire human catastrophe can be summed up in the simple word "more."

HOW COME IT'S BAD TO WATCH TV FOR HOURS BUT OKAY TO WATCH A FIRE?
94-25

WOULD IT BE OKAY TO SIT AND WATCH A FIRE IF IT WAS ON TV?

MAYBE ON THE EDUCATION CHANNEL?
THE DEEP IMPONDERABLES OF THE NORTH!
©D.URQUHART

Northerners watch a lot of television and, like everyone else, feel guilty about it. Years after I made this strip, I was channel surfing late at night in a hotel in Finland and one channel showed just a fire in a fireplace, with no music. Every 15 minutes or so a pair of tongs would place another log on the fire. Someone told me of a North American channel that did the same thing over Xmas and when it stopped there was a flood of complaints.

USE YOUR BACK EDDY!
USE YOUR BACK EDDY!
MARTEN'S TAKING KAYAK LESSONS..
I AM USING MY @** BACK!
94-26
AND MY NAME AIN'T **EDDY**!!
BUT HE HATES LEARNING FROM OUTSIDERS!
© D. URQUHART

Extreme sports are a facet of modern bush adventure that I find somewhat disturbing because the landscape merely becomes a challenging backdrop for the feat of daring. In the north this also becomes a bizarre paradox where northerners are increasingly less skilled in such outdoor activities than southerners.

TOURISM, MINING, CONSTRUCTION, FISH STOCKS, EVERYTHING IS DOWN!
WE NEED SOMETHING NEW TO STIMULATE OUR ECONOMY!

ABOMINABLE SNOWMAN?
TOO RISKY!
MUSH LAKE MONSTER?
TOO HARD!
LOST GOLD MINE?
DID THAT!
94-27

I'VE GOT IT! MEET ME AT BIRCH SWAMP TOMMORROW NIGHT!
© D. URQUHART
CONTINUED...

Northern communities are always looking for scams to make money and the gullibility of southerners is an obvious solution.

THIS MORNING RESIDENTS OF FT. DOGGEREL WOKE TO A PHENOMENON THAT DWARFS THE SENSATIONAL CROP CIRCLES OF EUROPE...
FT. DOGGEREL
©URQUHART

SCIENTISTS AND MEDIA ARE THRONGING TO A SWAMP NORTH OF THE TOWN TO INVESTIGATE THE WORLD'S FIRST...

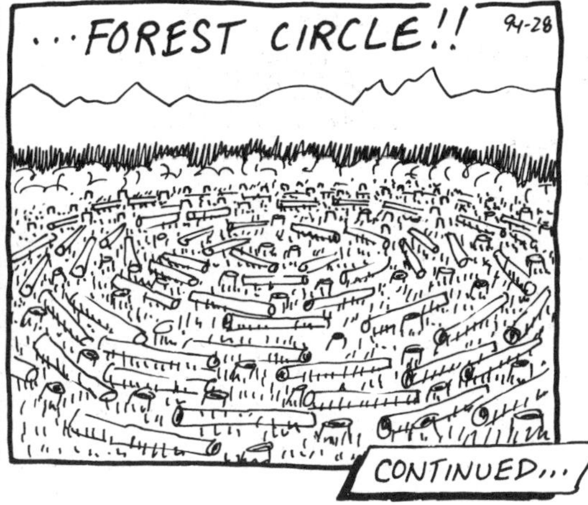
...FOREST CIRCLE!!
94-28
CONTINUED...

Crop circles were in the news at the time and there was much speculation about what produced them. My version is based on observations of die-offs in birch swamps that leave numerous rotten trunks held together only by the bark. They are thus easy and, in fact, fun to push over.

FT. DOGGEREL RESIDENT MARTEN FISHER REPORTED A BRIGHT LIGHT IN BIRCH SWAMP LAST NIGHT...
IT WAS WEIRD!
94-29
©D.URQUHART
...BUT WHEN HE GOT THERE, THE LIGHT WAS MOVING AWAY AT ASTONISHING SPEED!
UP! IT WENT UP!
MR. FISHER AND HIS FRIENDS ARE GRACIOUSLY RENTING ALL THEIR BUSH GEAR AND HAVE HIRED ON AS WELL TO HELP THE INVESTIGATION!
IT'S THE LEAST WE COULD DO!
CONTINUED...

I patterned this after the "Roswell" type documentaries where they interview amazingly inarticulate locals.

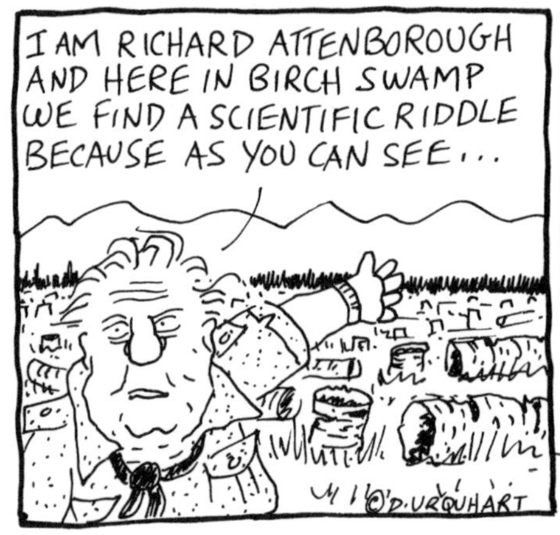
I AM RICHARD ATTENBOROUGH AND HERE IN BIRCH SWAMP WE FIND A SCIENTIFIC RIDDLE BECAUSE AS YOU CAN SEE...
©D.URQUHART

I AM KNEE DEEP IN MUCK WHICH RULES OUT HUMAN PRANKSTERS SINCE THEY WOULD HAVE LEFT NUMEROUS TRACKS SUCH AS I HAVE DONE...
94-30

UNLESS, OF COURSE, THEY WERE WEARING SNOWSHOES!!
CONTINUED...

This came from a current account of a young scientist who was tromping around northern sphagnum bogs on snowshoes in the middle of summer developing a theory about moss and global warming.

OKAY! THE FOREST CIRCLE GAG IS WINDING DOWN. WHAT DO WE DO NEXT?
WE NEED SOMETHING NOBODY HAS DONE BEFORE!
LIKE SOME REAL EVIDENCE?
94-31
©D.URQUHART

ANYONE REPORT THAT RUSSIAN SATELLITE THAT CRASHED ON VIC'S TRAPLINE?
AND HAVE THE FEDS ALL OVER US? NO WAY!

OKAY! BURN OFF ALL THE IDENTIFICATION AND WE'LL SALT IT WITH RARE METALS FROM OUR ASSAY SAMPLES!
CONTINUED...

In 1978, a Russian satellite crashed in the Northwest Territories east of Great Slave Lake. It caused quite a stir and parts were found by a party that had gone to the Thelon River to commemorate the death of the legendary Jack Hornby.

DISCOVERY OF WRECKAGE FROM AN ALIEN SPACECRAFT HAS EVERYONE FLOCKING BACK TO FT. DOGGEREL...
©D.URQUHART

BASED ON AN OBSCURE NORTHERN LAW, LOCALS CLAIM FULL POSSESSION AND ARE REFUSING CLOSE INSPECTION BY FEDERAL EXPERTS...

94-32
A LENGTHY COURT BATTLE WILL ENSUE, MEANWHILE DOGGEREL RESIDENTS HAVE THE OBJECT ON DISPLAY AND ARE CHARGING ADMISSION...
ALIEN MUSEUM
DANGER
ENTER HERE

The craft was powered by a nuclear generator that was supposed to incinerate on reentering the earth's atmosphere. But it didn't. Sophisticated equipment found radioactive material spread over 800 square miles around Hay River. One piece, a few centimetres long, would have quickly killed anyone who picked it up. The total clean-up cost was something like $11 million.

94-33
JUST A SECOND 'TIL I GET A FEW MORE SHOTS!
CLICK
CLICK
CLICK

OKAY! JUST HOLD THAT POT A LITTLE HIGHER!
CLICK
CLICK
CLICK
CLICK

SO? YOU HAVING A GOOD TIME?
GEE! I DUNNO!
CLICK
CL
CLICK
CLICK

I'LL HAVE TO WAIT 'TIL THE FILM IS DEVELOPED!
CLICK
CLICK
CLICK
©D.URQUHART

You see this tourist everywhere in the world. At the steaming rim of the Kilauea volcano in Hawaii, I saw a tourist lean over the guard rail into the rising vapours and snap a picture of the absolute blankness. What a memento!

WE SOLD EVERYTHING IN TAHOE AND MOVED HERE SO HARRY CAN WRITE HIS NOVEL AND I CAN SELL DRY FLOWER ARRANGEMENTS!

©D.URQUHART
6!
7½!
10!
WHAT ARE YOU DOING?

94-34
BETTING HOW MANY MONTHS BEFORE THEY EITHER SPLIT UP OR MOVE BACK SOUTH!

In small northern communities, there is a constant turnover of southerners who have fantasized about life in the north to the extent that they convince themselves to move up here – often sight unseen. These people usually arrive in the summer and come unglued during the long, dark, cold winter.

36 YEARS ON THIS CLAIM OLD COUTTS MUST'VE LEFT A STACHE OF NUGGETS!
AND I'LL CHECK THE DUMP FOR SOME GRUB!
RIP! SMASH! CRASH! BAM! CRUNCH!
I DON'T GET IT! WE TORE THIS PLACE APART AND NOT A FLAKE!
94-35
AND NO FOOD IN THE DUMP JUST A COFFEE TIN FULL OF YELLOW ROCKS!
© D. URQUHART

This was for an old prospector friend of mine. Bob Coutts was complaining to me one day about how people are always ransacking old cabins looking for caches of gold. Such windfalls are a popular northern myth, often exploited in fiction but rarely occurring in fact.

OH NO! I FORGOT TO HEM MY DRESS
I'LL DUCT TAPE IT!
© D. URQUHART
AND MY PURSE IS RIPPED!
DUCT TAPE!
AND MY COMPACT IS CRACKED!
DUCT TAPE!
AND MY BELT BUCKLE CAME OFF!
DUCT TAPE!
GEE! YOU LOOK GREAT ROSIE!
94-36
THANKS TO MY DUCT TAILOR!

This strip is based on my family life. Duct tape is a miracle solution, not only in the north, but everywhere that people are accustomed to doing things for themselves. Duct tape even saved Apollo 13.

THAT HOLLYWOOD CELEBRITY IS GETTING THE ROYAL TREATMENT FROM OUR LOCAL SNOBS!

TOUR OF THE LAKE AND BIG DINNER AT SLY BUCKMASTER'S FOLLOWED BY A WEEKEND AT HIS LODGE

YEP, TWO DAYS IN DOGGEREL
94-37

AND NEVER MET ONE REAL PERSON!
© D URQUHART

This is based on numerous observations of situations in northern communities, which, no matter how small, have a local snob class that commandeers any noteworthy visitor or special occasion, especially where media are involved.

HEY VERN SEE YOU TONIGHT? PAY DAY Y'KNOW?
YEAH VERN! PARTY LATER AT BARB'S!

94-38
YO! VERN! COMIN' BY THE LEGION?
YOU'RE PRETTY POPULAR, VERN!

YEAH! PLUS I'M A REFORMED ALCOHOLIC AND THEY ALL WANT
© D. URQUHART

A DESIGNATED DRIVER!

SO I'M GONNA PAINT THE BOAT AND CHANGE THE PROP...
BUT FIRST CLEAN THE DOG YARD!

THEN I'LL FIX THE CAMP STOVE AND THE TRAILER LIGHT!
BUT FIRST THE DOG YARD!

OKAY SKOOK! LET'S JUST SNEAK DOWN TO BUY SOME PLUGS!

94-39
BUT FIRST THE DOG YARD!
© D. URQUHART

WHAT ARE THEY DOING DAD?

STRAIGHTENING A BEND IN THE ROAD!
BUT WHY NOT BUILD IT STRAIGHT IN THE FIRST PLACE?
© D. URQUHART

BECAUSE THERE WOULD BE NOTHING FOR THEM TO DO FOR THE NEXT 50 YEARS.
94-40

I came across an old story about a group of men playing cards in the club car of a train crossing the United States in the early 1900s. Someone opened the door to the smoke-filled room and asked "Anyone here from the Yukon?" One of the card players nodded and the person said, "Great! Lend me your bottle opener!" Drinking used to be romantically synonymous with the frontier society of the north but this age is passing as our society tries to self correct.

This was a constant battle between my wife and myself for all the years we had dog teams. I guess men can just tolerate a lot more crap than women. Boy! Am I going to pay for this statement!

The northern highway repair season is relatively short. Ironically, the only time driving could be easy, it isn't — due to road construction and detours. Some of the best driving is on a well snow-packed road – one of the smoothest, quietest rides I know. Following trapline trails and other local paths, the Alaska Highway was pushed through in nine months during WWII.

INTRODUCING
SKOOKUM'S
TRUE STORIES FROM PAWS READERS
SEND TO: 61-13TH. AVE. WHITEHORSE YT. Y1A4K6
HEY! STOP THAT!
SITE M R.R.1
YECCH! THOSE ☆@✕ DOGS HAVE HOSED ALL THE LOWER BOXES!
SORRY BUT SECTION E OF THE POSTAL CODE STATES THAT RURAL DEPOTS CANNOT BE RAISED... HOWEVER, I MIGHT HAVE A SOLUTION...
©D.URQUHART
94-41
HE ASSIGNED US A HIGHER COMPARTMENT!

This was the beginning of what I thought would be a great way for northerners to share stories as I had already received a few such suggestions from readers. But as a strip feature it never got the response I was hoping for.

WHAT'S THAT STRANGE ANIMAL WITH YOU?
YOU DON'T KNOW ABOUT HUMANS?
THAT THEY HAVE CONQUERED THE WORLD AND POLLUTED THE ENVIRONMENT?
AND WIPED OUT LOTS OF SPECIES?
AND USE ANIMALS FOR EXPERIMENTS? AND TEAR UP THE LANDSCAPE?
SORRY! THEY DON'T COUNT FOR NUTHIN' IN THESE PARTS!
94-42
CAN I MOVE HERE?
©D.URQUHART

For several years my wife and I lived in a remote part of the bush where, prior to our arrival, most of the local wildlife had never seen humans before. A world without humans...would that be so bad?

OH NO! MORE ECO-FREAKS! WHAT'RE YOU MESSING UP THIS TIME? TRAPPING? HUNTING? WOLF CONTROL?

NOPE! WE MARCHED ON THE CAPITOL TO STOP CLEAR CUTTING IN THE RAGGED RANGE!
94-43

ULP! YOU GUYS SAVED MY TRAPLINE?
WHEN IS A GREENIE NOT AN ECO-FREAK? WHEN HE AGREES WITH YOU!
©D URQUHART

There is constant tension between many who make their living from the bush and those who are dedicated to wilderness protection. Ironically, these strongly held values often clash but at times work well together.

WE WERE INTRIGUED BY YOUR INVITATION TO A WORKSHOP ON ECONOMIC CONVERSION AND ENVIRONMENTAL PROTECTION!
©D. URQUHART

WE LOVE WORKSHOPS! ESCAPE THE OFFICE! FREE TRIPS GOOD FOOD! BUILD UP LIEU TIME!
94-44
GREAT! HERE IS MY WORKSHOP WHERE WE WILL

CONVERT MY 4×4 TO PROPANE TO SAVE MONEY AND THE ENVIRONMENT!

UH-OH! LOSING YOUR LEAVES SO SOON?!
SIGN OF OLD AGE WHEN YOU CAN'T HOLD YOUR LEAVES!
94-45

THEN THE ANTS START BORING IN YOUR TRUNK!
THEN BEETLES AND WOODPECKERS AND THEN A BIG WIND AND DOWN YOU GO!

TOUGH BEING THE LAST ASPEN ON THE RIDGE!!
©D. URQUHART

JUST ONE MORE TREE AND OUR NEW TRAIL WILL REACH THE ROAD!
94-46

NO! DON'T CUT IT!!!
SORRY! TOO LATE! WHY?
BRR-M-M-M
BRR-MM-MMM
©D. URQUHART

THAT'S WHY!
VAROOOM!

As a facilitator, I have to say that, as a means of problem solving, workshops can be either extremely valuable or highly abused. Often they are seen as an excuse for well paid bureaucrats to slack off. Conferences used to perform this function until government departments began prohibiting attendance at conferences. Suddenly major conferences became retitled as "workshops" and the bureaucrats were back in business.

This is the story of succession that I constantly see in the bush but instead of portraying it in a cold objective scientific way, I personalized it from the tree's viewpoint. When you live in the bush, everything takes on a personality and even your intellectual analysis of situations empathizes more and more with the plants and animals you share the land with.

Access is a growing problem in the north, occasioned by modern off-road vehicles and the way they've invaded what was once the private domain of the fortunate few who lived and worked in the bush. As a member of the Yukon Fish and Wildlife Management Board, I am in a group trying to protect wildlife habitats from these disturbances. A frequent complaint comes from trappers who cut new lines but can't limit their use by others whose presence then disturbs their trapping activities.

OKAY FRITZ WE GOT BEAR BELLS!
YA! TINKLE TINKLE!
UNT BEAR SPRAY!
YA! FIZZ FIZZ!
UNT BIG BEAR GUN!
YA! BOOM BOOM
UNT SAFETY WHISTLE!
TWEET! TWEET!
UNT FLARE GUN?
WHOOSH!
UNT EMERGENCY BEACON?
BEEP! BEEP!
94-47
WELL FRITZ!
YA?
ARE WE READY TO GO TO THE OUTHOUSE?
CAMPGROUND
SIGN IN
©D. URQUHART

I was staying at the Tombstone Campground on the Dempster Highway a few years ago when I first heard, then saw, a couple of European tourists walking along an interpretive trail all decked out in the most fantastic adventure gear imaginable, including bear bells.

SO? HOW WAS YOUR TRIP?
TERRIBLE! I WISH I HAD NEVER SEEN THIS COUNTRY!!
94-48
GEE! THAT GUY REALLY HATES THE NORTH!
NOPE! HE JUST FOUND OUT...
...WHAT HE'D BEEN MISSING HIS WHOLE LIFE!!
©D. URQUHART

Driving along the Dempster Highway, which has some of the most beautiful scenery in the world, I often feel grateful that I made the decision to move north so early in life. What if I had discovered this place only later and missed all those great years of my youth?

SKOOKUM'S
TRUE STORIES
FROM 'PAWS' READERS
SEND TO:
61 - 13TH. AVE.
WHITEHORSE
Y.T. Y1A 4K6
94-49
BOY! THAT WAS SURE A ROUGH CROSSING!
BANG!
BANG!
BANG!
WHERE'S THE FRYING PAN?
RIGHT HERE (ULP!) ON TOP OF THE DISHES!!
©D. URQUHART

This story is based on a letter I received. As I said, the feature resulted in very few responses.

1994

SORRY! MARTEN! THAT LAKE'S TOO SMALL
NO WAY! I LANDED HERE LAST YEAR!
OKAY! IF YOU SAY SO!
ROAR! CRASH! BUMP! BUMP! CRUNCH!!
94-50
DANG! SAME THING HAPPENED LAST TIME!
PILOT RULE #1 NEVER LISTEN TO THE PASSENGER!

This is a joke told to me by a dentist friend who used to "chisel charter" on Haida Gwai (Queen Charlotte Islands). As a survey biologist, flying hundreds of hours counting muskox and caribou, I have had several such experiences.

LAST LOAD AND I'LL COME BACK FOR YOU!
DON'T FORGET NOW!

HEY RITA! THISH IS A..A GREAT (URP!) PARDY!
YAH! IT WAS SUPPOSED TO BE FOR MARTEN FISHER'S BIRTHDAY

94-51
BUT HE NEVER SHOWED UP!

HAPPY BIRTHDAY TO ME...

There are numerous stories along this line in the north. I was surveying caribou on an arctic island in the early 1970s when my pilot dropped me off at a seismic camp and went back the 200 miles to the community to refuel. He ran into a party there, got homesick and hopped the scheduled flight down south to his family in Saskatchewan. I waited in vain at the camp for several days until I finally hitched a ride back to town on the company's Twin Otter.

GEE! YOUR GEAR SURE ROLLS UP NEAT!!
YES! EVERYTHING FITS TIGHT AS A GLOVE!!!
94-52
© D. URQUHART

EXCEPT WHEN YOU'RE PACKING THEM ANYWHERE OUTSIDE THE ☆◎✳ CAMPING STORE!!!

This happens to everybody. It would simplify things immensely if manufacturers would just make bigger stuff sacks. I fall for this myself. The little bag looks so cute in the trendy outdoor store, and packs so well on the soft carpet. Most camp gear fits better in green garbage bags.

Time

1995

WELL ANOTHER MONDAY IN THE BUSH AND NO CLOCK TO PUNCH!
IT'S NOT MONDAY IT'S WEDNESDAY!

Life in the bush follows a different world of time. First you lose the hour of the day, then the day of the week, then the week of the month and, finally, the months themselves give way to seasons. Meanwhile, other realities take on greater meaning - like a song bird who lives only a couple of years, a moose that may reach 20, and trees and rocks and lakes that span many human lifetimes.

UH-OH! LOSING YOUR LEAVES SO SOON?!
SIGN OF OLD AGE WHEN YOU CAN'T HOLD YOUR LEAVES!
94-45

160 MILLION YEARS FOR EROSION TO PUT ME ON A MOUNTAIN TOP IN THE SUN!!
©D. URQUHART
95-19

1995

HERE WE GO IN OUR 4x4 MOOSE HUNTING! MOOSE HUNTING!
BLAM! BLAM! BLAM!
HERE WE GO IN OUR 4x4 CARIBOU HUNTING! CARIBOU HUNTING!
©D.URQUHART
95-1

YES! THE GRAY JAYS SHOULD BE CHARGED FOR STEALING YOUR SPECIAL BANNOCK WITH RAISINS IN IT!
©D.URQUHART

WE'LL CALL A FOREST COUNCIL TONIGHT AND THE RAVEN CAN BE OUR LAWYER!
95-2

THE JAYS CAN HAVE THE EAGLE BECAUSE (FRANKLY) HE'S **A DOPE!**

SHE NEEDS TO GET OUT!
AND SOON!

AH! A SIMPLE BUSH LUNCH AWAY FROM THE HURLY BURLY OF THE WORLD!
©D.URQUHART

WITH AN ORANGE FROM FLORIDA, BREAD FROM THE PRAIRIES AND TUNA FROM KOREA!
BANANA FROM COSTA RICA CHEESE FROM HOLLAND, TEA FROM CEYLON AND GERMAN SAUSAGE!
95-3

GEE! EVEN LUNCH IN THE BUSH HAS BECOME AN INTERNATIONAL EVENT!

Road hunters are a notorious breed in the north. Such hunting is very opportunistic and not highly regarded for skill or experience. Recently, a friend of mine in the Yukon did some wildlife surveying in an area where the moose were reputed to be declining. He found a significant correlation between moose density and distance from roads, leading him to believe that the moose were just being reduced locally by road hunters and were doing fine elsewhere.

When my wife and I lived full time in the bush without seeing other people for months at a time, the other animals and plants became our "community". Making up silly little stories for our amusement became a daily pastime. Individuals who have no other society may take this to the extreme where they become "bushed." A bushed trapper named Gunter Lichy attacked me once. He was killed by an even more bushed person, "Sheslay Mike" who, in turn, was killed by the cops.

When I was a young prospector in northern Ontario and Quebec I used to marvel at the exotic food we'd have every day for lunch. Such a contrast from the country we were in and what it could provide! A few decades earlier, an orange for lunch in the bush would have been an exotic luxury.

95-4
WE CAME NORTH TO ESCAPE THE MATERIALISM OF THE SOUTH, RAMPANT CONSUMERISM AND WORSHIP OF WORLDLY POSSESSIONS

TEN YEARS AGO WE ARRIVED WITH ALL OUR BELONGINGS IN TWO PACKSACKS ON OUR BACKS...

©D. URQUHART
AND NOW I CAN'T EVEN FIND THE @☆✱ BACKPACKS!

After a spell of travelling, my wife and I came back to the north, literally with two packsacks. Twenty years later, we have 4 houses, 4 vehicles, 4 boats, 2 kids and a dog. And we are always talking about simplifying our lives.

NOTHING TO DO... NOTHING TO DO...

YOU LOOK BORED SKOOK! HERE'S A BIG BONE!
GEE! THANKS!
©D. URQUHART

95-5
NOTHING TO DO... NOTHING TO DO...

Dogs are like people. They are people. Many dogs have a terrible time trying to amuse themselves. I have known dogs in northern towns who have every form of freedom and yet can't think of anything to do. If they were humans they would watch TV. Other dogs are on the go from dawn to dark – and after dark!

WE DON'T KNOW MUCH ABOUT EARLY PEOPLE HERE BUT...

95-6
WE CAN TELL A LOT FROM THEIR MIDDENS!
YOU MEAN YOU FOUND SOME?

YES! AND THEY ARE MORE THAN 10,000 YEARS OLD!!

GOSH! THOSE EARLY PEOPLE SURE COULD KNIT!!
©D. URQUHART

This is my friend Gary Kofinas again who was a PhD student in the northern Yukon for a number of years. Unlike most of his ilk, he has stayed around and become very popular in the communities. Whenever I need an "academic" for a character, I think of him, and in certain research circles this caricature is making him famous. A midden is a domestic refuse heap which may be anything from broken pottery to clam shells, bones, etc.

HURRY! THE SNORTING BEAST IS GAINING ON US!!!
95-7
MAYBE WE SHOULD JUMP OFF THE TRAIL?

ARE YOU CRAZY? IF IT'S THIS FAST ON THE TRAIL...

IT WILL CATCH US FOR SURE IN THE DEEP SNOW!!
HONK!!
HOOONK!!
©D.URQUHART

This is a joke I heard from a Gwich'in hunter at a meeting of the Porcupine Caribou Management Board at the Eagle Plains Hotel on the Dempster Highway in 1986. Caribou are a frequent road hazard on this arctic highway. In winters with deep snow, they use the road for travel but when they get surprised by transport trucks on the way to Inuvik, they are afraid to jump off to safety.

WHEN MY GREAT GRANDPA CAME HERE, THERE WAS NOTHING BUT WILDERNESS!

AND BEING AN ENERGETIC YOUNG MAN FROM A BIG INDUSTRIAL FAMILY BACK EAST...

HE MADE A DECISION THAT AFFECTED THIS ENTIRE REGION!
95-8

©D.URQUHART
HE LEFT IT ALONE!

This is a typical "gag" set up where you lead people along a classic train of thought and reverse the ending. It's basically a satire on how things usually transpire but there truly are people like this who come to conquer the north and fall in love with it instead.

AS CHAIRMAN OF THE WILDLIFE COUNCIL I SAY NO ROAD IN THIS VALLEY!
95-9
BUT AS CHAIR OF THE BOARD OF TRADE I SAY YES!
©D.URQUHART

AS CHAIR OF THE HERITAGE COMMITTEE I MUST OPPOSE YOU!
BUT AS CHAIR OF THE VILLAGE COUNCIL I MUST SUPPORT IT!

OKAY! NO ROAD!
AND NO $700 A DAY FACILITATOR!

Small northern villages are pocket-sized countries in a way. All the major positions of authority must be filled by a handful of people. I had one friend in Mayo who, for a while, had three desks in three different buildings.

ACTUALLY THAT WAS ON THE PBS SPECIAL AND THE 48 HOURS VERSION NEVER COVERED THAT ASPECT OF THE ISSUE

OF COURSE THE BEST IN DEPTH COVERAGE WAS THE A&E 10 PART SERIES BUT I LIKE CBS MORE!
©D.URQUHART

YAH! THAT COMES ON AFTER ROSEANNE RIGHT?
GEE! I WOULDN'T KNOW MARTEN!

95-10
WE HARDLY EVER WATCH TV!!
AND NOBODY READS THE NATIONAL ENQUIRERER

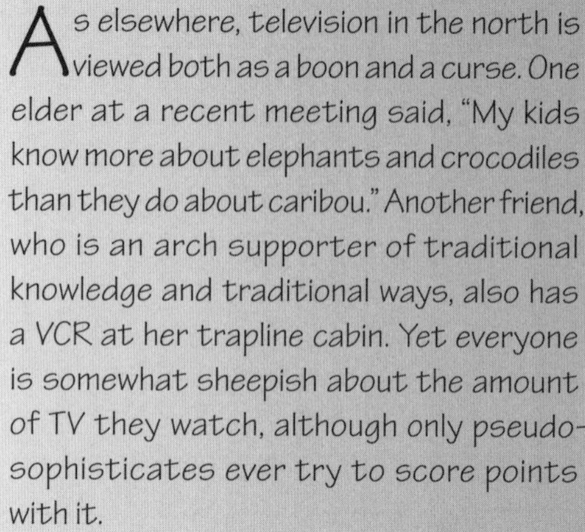

As elsewhere, television in the north is viewed both as a boon and a curse. One elder at a recent meeting said, "My kids know more about elephants and crocodiles than they do about caribou." Another friend, who is an arch supporter of traditional knowledge and traditional ways, also has a VCR at her trapline cabin. Yet everyone is somewhat sheepish about the amount of TV they watch, although only pseudo-sophisticates ever try to score points with it.

DID YOU SEE THE NOTICE IN THE POST OFFICE?
ABOUT THE HIGHWAY COMING TO TOWN?

YEAH! FROM SOME PLACE CALLED 'INFORMATION'!
I'D BETTER BUY SVEN'S CAT AND WELD UP THE LOADER!

95-11
GOVERNMENT GUY'S COMING TOMORROW. WE CAN ASK HIM ABOUT CONTRACTS!
THEN THEY'LL STRANGLE HIM WITH HIS OWN MODEM CORD!

When the Internet first arrived in the north, the buzz phrase on every bureaucrat's lips was "The Information Highway" and vast sums were spent getting the communities plugged in. This is what happens when southern jargon gets way ahead of northern communities. Computers are still viewed with suspicion by many die-hard bush types.

LET'S GET THIS STRAIGHT! YOU JUST HELPED A GUY YOU ARGUED WITH IN THE BAR LAST NIGHT?

HE'S FROM DOGGEREL!

GREAT! THEN ANYONE FROM THE CITY SHOULD HELP ME?
NOPE!

95-12
YOU'RE NOT FROM DOGGEREL!
WHY NOT?
THE "NORTHERN BROTHERHOOD" A SOUTHERN CONUNDRUM!
©D.URQUHART

Community bonds are very strange in little northern villages. For years I had an adversarial relationship with an elderly resident of our community. Then one day he came over and asked me to make some posters advertising renovations he was planning for our park. I was stunned and, moreover, not in favour of the modifications. But he had asked me and I thought, "What the hell! It's the north!" so I did it.

NOTICE HOW I CONSTANTLY TRY TO SUCEED AND MAKE A MARK IN THE WORLD?

REACH FOR THE TOP! STRIVE TO SUCCEED! WINNING IS EVERYTHING! THOSE ARE MY MOTTOS AND SHOULD BE YOURS!
ZAK!
95-13
ON THE OTHER HAND BE HUMBLE, ENJOY LIFE AND SIMPLE PLEASURES SOUNDS PRETTY GOOD TOO!
©D. URQUHART

MY GOD! ALIENS! WHAT'LL WE DO?
LEAVE IT TO ME!

HURRY! TAKE OFF QUICK! THIS PLANET HAS HUGE METAL BEASTS THAT EAT EVERYTHING!
©D. URQUHART

THERE GOES ONE NOW! SEE! WITH TWO VICTIMS IN IT'S BELLY!!
95-14

WE JUST SAVED THE WORLD BUT DON'T TELL MARTEN! OK?

$190 IS A LOT FOR A PAIR OF MOCCASINS!
OH YEAH? THOSE ARE 2 DAYS WORK WHICH IF I WAS A COMPUTER CONSULTANT LIKE YOU WOULD BE $900!!!

©D. URQUHART
SO? DID YOU GET A PAIR?
ARE YOU KIDDING? AT THOSE PRICES...

95-15
I BOUGHT 3 PAIRS!!!

Here's a paraphrase of a central Taoist tenet, "The Wise Man, therefore, while he is alive, will never make a show of being great: And that is how his greatness is achieved." In 1976, on the eve of a round-the-world trip, I was given a copy of the *Tao Te Ching* by a very weird guy named Steve. After three years in the bush, the book, constructed basically on paradoxes between social norms and mystic insights of hermits who rejected society, made excellent sense.

The key to Einstein's Theory of Relativity is his dispensing with the earth as a frame of reference and showing that space and time are not constant but only "relative" to the frame of reference. Cartoonists (and schizophrenics) are always changing their frame of reference. For people like us, staying in touch with the everyday frame of reference or "reality" is the big challenge. In this strip I changed the frame of reference to a plausible "aliens" interpretation.

This cartoon is already way out of date. She should be saying "$2000!" The amount of work and skill in making such products bears no resemblance to the price they command. It's just a sign of the times. A few generations ago, an Inuit hunter who could not find a female partner to keep up with the sewing was as good as dead.

WELL SKOOK YOU'VE SIRED A COUPLE OF LITTERS EVERY YEAR FOR THE PAST 10 YEARS!

AT ABOUT 6 PUPS PER LITTER AND IF EACH PUP PRODUCED A LITTER OR TWO A YEAR...
© D. URQUHART

95-16
WHICH IS WHY THIS TOWN IS OVERRUN BY MORE THAN 5,000 HUSKIES!!!
SO HOW ARE DOGS SUPPOSED TO KNOW ABOUT GEOMETRIC PROGRESSION!

The real lesson of geometric progression is the ability of species like rabbits or wolves to make sudden comebacks from near extirpation. At a workshop on wolf control, I said that depressing a wolf population is not as risky as it looks because they can "bounce back" so fast. This apparently did not translate well into "Kaska" because one of the elders asked the translator, "What are they doing now? Dropping wolves out of planes!"

SO, LET'S LET THAT ISSUE SIMMER ON A BACK BURNER AND PUT THE HEAT ON OUR BIG PROJECT!
© D. URQUHART

THEN WE CAN PREPARE OUR NEXT MOVE FOR WHEN THE OTHERS ARE DONE!

95-17
GEE ROSIE! HOW COME YOU'RE SO GOOD AT JUGGLING PROGRAMS AND RESOURCES?
EASY!

I COOK ON A WOOD STOVE!

Cooking on a woodstove is an art form that I watched my wife perfect. Choosing the kind of wood, the size of the pieces, knowing where the hot spots are and moderating the oven temperature constitutes a complex strategy to yield a product. In mulling this over, I realized that such terms are often applied to big business and probably arose from a former era where they had relevance. The art in cartooning is to take a social observation and express it in an imaginative way.

I SAW LIZ RIDING IN ROY'S TRUCK!
SO WHAT?
95-18

I SAW LIZ AND HER DOGS RIDING IN ROY'S TRUCK!
WELL, THEY ARE FRIENDS

I SAW LIZ'S DOGS RIDING IN ROY'S TRUCK WITHOUT LIZ!

THEY'RE SHACKED UP!
© D. URQUHART

Anyone from a small town will instantly recognize this. It begins with rumours that a couple has split up, followed by reports of seeing one of the partners in someone else's vehicle. But this alone is not conclusive evidence. The dogs, however, will clinch it. I favour short names because they save space in the speech bubbles.

160 MILLION YEARS FOR EROSION TO PUT ME ON A MOUNTAIN TOP IN THE SUN!!
©D. URQUHART
95-19

HEY SKOOK! THIS SHOULD MAKE A REAL BIG SPLASH!!
OKAY SO ANOTHER 30 MILLION YEARS TO DRAIN THIS LAKE AND I'LL BE IN A NICE SUNNY VALLEY!

Rolling rocks is a wonderful bush pastime that I have happily engaged in throughout my life. As a young prospector's assistant learning about the incredible time frames for geological change, I used to muse on the sudden transformation our little amusement was having on the rocks we would roll. One year, a young prospecting acquaintance of mine rolled a mighty boulder down a steep overhang and took out the bottom of his canoe.

OH LOOK AT ALL THOSE DAFFODILS!
AND THE HYACINTHS!
©D. URQUHART

95-20
AND THE LEAVES ARE IN BUD!!
OH! WAS THAT A BUTTERFLY?

SPRING TIME ON A SOUTHERN CHANNEL!

My wife has done this for years. It usually happens during a newscast where the reporter is outside, with a city park backdrop, and my wife will begin oooing and ahhing about the flowers. This begins in early February and goes on until about early April when the end of winter comes to our home.

HURRY SKOOK! THE COMMUNITY ELECTIONS ARE TONIGHT!
95-21
GEE MARTEN! YOU'RE SO AMBITIOUS!!

YOU DON'T KNOW THIS TOWN! IF YOU'RE NOT THERE IN PERSON!!

THEY'LL ELECT YOU TO EVERYTHING!!
©D. URQUHART
CONGRATULATIONS MARTEN! YOU'RE CHAIRMAN AND HEAD OF ALL THE COMMITTEES!!

This is a common joke in the north and is set up as a paradox with my southern stooge Hal who interprets everything from a southern viewpoint. Experienced northern residents shy away from any responsible posting because they have already had so much experience with such jobs before. Thus, there is no allure left, whereas in the south, average people rarely get a chance to occupy positions of authority.

STRANGE TRACKS! WEBBED PATTERN SHORT WADDLING STRIDE, HEAVY BODY,...
IS IT DANGEROUS?
95-22

NO! FROM THIS DATA I DEDUCE IT TO BE A VERY LARGE FLIGHTLESS BIRD OF NO THREAT TO OUR SAFETY!
AMAZING! ALL THAT JUST FROM TRACKS!

HEY! AFTER ALL I'M A TRAINED SCIENTIST!!!
©D.URQUHART

A few springs ago I was startled to find a large webbed track in the bush. Turned out to be an errant goose that had landed briefly in a clearing about 3 weeks ahead of schedule. If it had been later in the year or nearer water there would have been no problem, but as it was, my "scientific brain" could not find a solution. From that episode to the cartoon is just a typical "daydream" for the average cartooning satirist.

WELL ANOTHER MONDAY IN THE BUSH AND NO CLOCK TO PUNCH!
IT'S NOT MONDAY IT'S WEDNESDAY!

95-23
CAN'T BE! WE'VE BEEN HERE 11 WEEKS TODAY!!
12 AND A HALF WEEKS!

BUT IT'S STILL FEBRUARY!!
NOPE IT'S MARCH!
WHEN THEY GET TO WHAT YEAR IT IS I'M OUTTA HERE!

There are two kinds of bush experience. The common kind is where your head never leaves town because you are only "visiting" for a short while. The other kind is when you live in the bush for extended periods with no commitments back in civilization. In this case you quickly lose track of artificial chronologies. My wife and I have often found ourselves listening intently to the radio trying to resolve a dispute about what day or even what month it is.

3 MONTHS LIVING THE PURE LIFE IN THE BUSH...
©D.URQUHART

NOTHING BUT COUNTRY FOOD LIKE MOOSE, FISH, BERRIES...
I FOUND IT! I FOUND IT!
WHAT?
95-24
A WHOLE OH HENRY CHOCOLATE BAR!
OHENRY

When we lived in the bush we got resupplied only once or twice a year. Our daily fare became pretty mundane – moose and dried vegetables, caribou and dried vegetables, grouse and dried vegetables, grayling and dried vegetables. At night, my wife would dream of "fresh" foods only to wake to moose and dried vegetables. Under such circumstances, silly little items were hoarded like gold.

THEN THERE'S THE GUY WHO BOUGHT SNOW TIRES BUT...
95-25

BEFORE HE GOT THEM ON THE CAR THEY MELTED!!
HAR!
HAR!
HAR!
THAT'S NOT SO FUNNY!

THE SAME THING HAPPENED TO ME!

This is an old joke that goes with the one about the guy who went ice fishing and caught 20 pounds of ice. I'm proud of the expressions on Marten's and the other guy's face which is the shared "look" that insiders give to each other in the presence of a fool.

THAT'S THE MOOSE BIOLOGIST, WATERFOWL BIOLOGIST, FURBEARER BIOLOGIST, RAPTOR BIOLOGIST, HABITAT BIOLOGIST, MARINE BIOLOGIST, FISH BIOLOGIST...

IF THAT'S BIODIVERSITY THEY CAN SHOVE IT!!
95-26

Nowadays a government wildlife unit is virtually indistinguishable from any other open space office complex. You can't tell the various biologists from each other except by inference from the posters on their cubicle dividers. Ironically, it is the advanced thinking of such people that has lead to the modern management concepts of conserving and fostering diversity in the natural environment.

ANOTHER FLAT AND MY SPARE'S BACK AT MARTEN'S!!
HERE! TAKE MY TRUCK!!

BUT YOU DON'T EVEN KNOW ME!
95-27
I SEEN YOU PLENTY 'ROUND DOGGEREL!

I DID IT!!
I'M A NORTHERNER!
©D. URQUHART

This is Hal's one moment of glory. Becoming a familiar face is a big step on the road to acceptance in a small community. My anthropology friend Gary once wrote a paper titled, "Don't do anything for a month after you get there," which was advice to researchers to just hang out in a community for a while before trying to start any study program.

WOULD YOU CARE TO SIGN THIS PETITION AGAINST GUNS AND HUNTING?
95-28
OH!

I GUESS NOT!!
FISHER
©D. URQUHART

The anti-gun or gun registration lobby has had a very rough ride in the north where guns and hunting are part of everyday life. Most of us have yet to register our firearms in the faint hope that the legislation will somehow be rescinded due to court challenges.

MARTEN IS GUIDING AN ANIMAL RIGHTS GROUP TO PROTEST THE WOLF CONTROL
STOP THE SLAUGHTER
SAVE THE WOLF

BUT HE'S HOPING TO SHOW THEM THAT NATURE AT LEAST WORKS BOTH WAYS
HERE'S THE REMAINS OF A MOOSE CALF SOME WOLF KILLED
SAVE THE WOLF
STOP SLAU

95-29
KILL THE WOLF! KILL THE WOLF!!
BUT WITH SOME PEOPLE YOU JUST CAN'T WIN!!

Environmentalists are an essential part of our society and they often do a lot of good. But extreme factions have little support here where people appreciate the complexities of northern ecosystems for which there are no simple answers.

SKOOKUM'S NORTHERN HERITAGE COURSE
"THE SUMMER HARVEST"

IN LATE SPRING A SMALL BOY IS POSTED AS LOOKOUT ON THE HIGHEST HILL...

MEANWHILE THE VILLAGERS MAKE READY WHILE WAITING FOR THE CALL...
THEY'RE COMING!!!
"TOURIST SEASON"
95-30
SMOKED SALMON
WILDLIFE CARVINGS
CRAFTS
WELCOME TO FORT DOGGEREL

I once camped south of Coppermine with some Inuit families who were waiting for the return of the Bathurst Caribou Herd. Every day, the children would stare across the tundra, then throw up their hands and, like their parents, sigh, "Tuktu beziak!" "No caribou!" Our annual preparations for the tourist season somewhat resemble a hunting society. The territorial tourism motto used to be "Attract, Hold and Satisfy" which sounded to me like someone was getting screwed.

1995

95-31
AHH! ALONE AGAIN IN THE BUSH WITH NOBODY ELSE AROUND!
EIN ZWIE! EIN ZWIE! EIN ZWIE! EIN ZWIE!
ADVANCED STAGE OF WILDERNESS DENIAL!

A Gwich'in friend of mine from Old Crow met some German tourists who had come from Inuvik, over the Rat Pass and down the Porcupine River in an astonishingly short period of time. Often they materialize, armed with cameras looking for "native festivities," and are as quickly gone again when nothing picturesque is forthcoming. Northerners who pride themselves on their ability to survive in the harsh wilderness find sudden encounters with such adventurers unnerving.

WINCH! I THINK WE'RE LOST!!!

95-32
NEVER MIND! MY DAD SAYS I HAVE A 6TH SENSE IN THE BUSH!!!
©D. URQUHART

THEN WE'RE DOOMED YOU DUMMY! THAT WAS LAST SUMMER!
Doggerel

NOW YOU'RE SEVEN!!

Kids can be so literal. One year, I showed my young son and daughter a flock of geese migrating south, explaining the aerodynamics of the "V" formation and adding that the birds were on their way back to Vancouver (where we had seen them the previous winter). My son pondered this for a moment and then asked, "Dad, when they fly north next spring to Atlin will they be in an "A" formation?"

95-33
DID YOU KNOW WE EVOLVED FROM FISH THAT GREW ARMS AND LEGS?
HOW COME?

EVOLUTION! SURVIVAL OF THE FITTEST! THE ONLY FISH TO REACH THE SPAWNING GROUNDS WERE THE ONES THAT...
COULD CLIMB THE FISH LADDERS!!
RABID RIVER FISH LADDER
©D. URQUHART

As with the previous strip, this one is based on a kid's simplification of a very complex relationship. One day I was wearing a T-shirt that said, "Proud to be Gwich'in" and underneath "Gwich'in Nation." My daughter read it and sometime later asked what being "Gwich" was. When I asked what she meant, she said my T-shirt read, "Proud to be Gwich in Gwich'in Nation."

THE ARROW'S BACK!
95-34
THE ARROW?
YEP SUMMER IS REALLY HERE!
WHAT'S THE ARROW? A FLOCK OF GEESE? SNOWMELT PATTERN? TRADITIONAL KNOWLEDGE?
WHAT THEN?
©D. URQUHART
NOPE! NOPE! NOPE!
SUMMER'S OFFICIALLY HERE WHEN THEY PUT UP THE ARROW ON THE FIRE SIGN!
FIRE HAZARD
NIL LOW MED HIGH

Every fall in Atlin and in the Yukon, the Forest Service takes the arrows down from all its fire hazard signs. Do they think someone is going to steal them? Or are they so tied to bureaucracy that without a printed index from their equipment they feel that to leave the arrow at "Low" all winter would be lying? Anyway, when the arrow goes up you know spring is over in the north!

AH! THE PRISTINE NORTH! CLEAR SKIES! CLEAN AIR! THE PERFECT PLACE FOR YOU TO QUIT SMOKING!
YOU'RE RIGHT I QUIT!!
©D. URQUHART
95-35
ONE SMALL BUTT FOR A MAN... A GIANT LEAP FOR HUMANS AND NATURE!
TO BE CONTINUED

In 1998, the federal government spent $22 million fighting forest fires in the Yukon. All of the major fires were human caused. I wanted to do a series on forest fires and this was the introductory strip.

ANOTHER FIRE JUST CALLED IN
95-36
YEAH? SO?
AT JACKFISH LAKE!
CALL THE SPOTTER PLANES! FIRE UP THE BOMBERS! FILL THE TANKERS! LOAD THE CATS! GATHER THE GRUBHOES, SHOVELS, TENTS, CHAINSAWS! PISS PUMPS! ROUNDUP THE BARFLIES!

THAT'S MY TRAPLINE!
THOUGHT HE'D BE INTERESTED!
TO BE CONTINUED

Much of my earliest experience with trappers and dog teams comes from the time I was a game officer in Ft. Smith, which is on the NWT/Alberta border. One local trapper showed me how to run dogs and a fellow officer instructed me in net fishing under the ice. Several years later, a massive fire wiped out all the traplines in the area I had become familiar with.

OUR FAMILY TRAPLINE IS BURNING!
SORRY MARTEN BUT IT'S TOO REMOTE AND WE GOT TO FIGHT THE MOOSE BERRY FIRE!!
FOREST FIRE IS PART OF NATURE AND THE BUSH WILL COME BACK!

YEAH! IN ABOUT 130 YEARS!!

One summer I found evidence that fire fighters had put out a spot fire near the cabin that my wife and I built 25 years ago and have used ever since. My family is eternally grateful to those anonymous youngsters. Fire ecology, that is, purposely setting fires to improve wildlife habitats, is a "hot" issue in the north. Bush fires make great sense in theory but take a terrible personal toll wherever they occur.

FT. DOGGEREL FISH DERBY
1992
1993
1994
1995
DO YOU THINK WE'RE OVER FISHING THE LAKE?

As a member of the Yukon Fish and Wildlife Management Board, I observe frequent controversies about overfishing. Sometimes the evidence, like in this strip, is overwhelming but still some people can't accept a fact that is going to change their personal lifestyles.

SIGH! MORE CITY SLICKER TOURISTS!!
HI THERE! WE'RE FROM CHESAPEAKE BAY AND... WHOA! IS THAT RANDY??

HEY! THE WATSONS! SO! YOU MADE IT!
YOU BET! AFTER ALL YOUR STORIES WE HAD TO SEE THE NORTH!

SO? HOW'S ABOUT SOME COFFEE?

Of all northern wildlife, migratory birds experience the greatest variety of environments. Tundra swans come to the Yukon from as far away as Chesapeake Bay near Washington, D.C. I used this to challenge the smugness of northerners who think they know everything about wildlife and that southerners are completely ignorant. Also, this is an example of how friendships can form with tourists.

WELL, HERE COME OUR CHEECHAKOS BACK FROM THE WORTHLESS CLAIM WE SOLD THEM!
PLUS ALL THE GEAR AND TOOLS

SO FRITZ AND HERMAN! FIND LOTS OF GOLD OUT THERE? (heh, heh)
YA! ZUM NOOGITS VEE ZINK!

95-40
THE KLONDIKE GOLD RUSH REVISITED!

Most placer miners consider themselves experts and many are quick to ridicule the naïve. Even during the 1898 gold rush some "cheechakos" (newcomers) staked so-called "worthless ground" and made a fortune. I enjoy parodying Germans because their confidence and enthusiasm often gets them into (and out of) amazing predicaments.

THANK GOD! A TRAIL! WE'RE SAFE!
IT'S GOING THE WRONG WAY!

BUT IT'S BETTER THAN SLOGGING THROUGH THE BUSH ON A **HUNCH**!!
OKAY! YOU FOLLOW THE TRAIL AND I'LL FOLLOW **MY HUNCH!**

95-41
SHUT UP!

A true bushman navigates by the lay of the land and clues that an outsider would never notice. A classic example is the Inuit polar bear hunters who regularly travel many miles on the sea ice far from sight of land with no apparent means of navigation. On the other hand, there is the joke about the oldtimer who stated confidently that he had never been lost in the bush but occasionally "confused" for a few days.

WHAT ARE YOU DOING HERE?
OVERCROWDING AT HOME AND THE OTHER MARSHES ARE DRAINED FOR HOUSING DEVELOPMENTS
95-42

SIGH! AN ACE TRAPPER AND INTREPID HUSKY RESCUING A YOUNG BUCK BEAVER FROM URBAN SPRAWL

OH WELL! IT'S **THE NINETIES!**
©D. URQUHART

Urban encroachment is a force of change even in the north. I coupled this with the fact that at two years of age, beavers must leave the home pond and seek new territory. Thus they sometimes wind up in odd places. With the decline of the trapping industry and traditional lifestyles, beavers are becoming more numerous than ever before. I recently did beaver management workshops in Carmacks and Pelly Crossing where beaver are interfering with salmon and whitefish spawning.

HUMANS ARE SUCH WOOSIES!

WHEN IT'S COLD YOU NEED INSULATED SHOEPACKS WHEN ITS WET YOU NEED BIG RUBBER BOOTS BUT HUSKIES ONLY NEED...
© D'URQUHART
95-43

THEIR TOUGH AND TRUSTY PAWS FOR ANY KIND OF WEATHER!

In the north, spring break-up, in particular, is a period of terrible muddy conditions. At such times we ambush our dog as he tries to scoot past into the house so we can clean his feet. He always submits with an impatient air that clearly shows he has no idea why we are doing this strange thing.

HOLD THE FORT DOG!
95-44

FORT DOG... FORT DOGGEREL.... FORT DOG-GIRL... DOG-GIRL... DOG-BOY...

HEY VIC! DOG-BOY SAYS "HOLD THE FORT DOG-GIRL! GET IT?

© D.URQUHART
MARTEN YOU'RE SPENDING TOO MUCH TIME IN THE BUSH!!

My dog travels everywhere with me on errands during the day. I often say this to him when I am leaving the truck and this led to the daydream Marten has. I searched for a suitable ending and chose the common "bushed" theme.

OKAY MY TURN! NOW WHEN MARTEN SITS HERE THE TRUCK MOVES!

MAYBE THIS STICK DOES... ALL RIGHT!
©D.URQUHART
CLICK!

95-45
SHOULDN'T YOU HAVE YOUR PAWS ON THAT WHEEL?
NAH! IT'S JUST FOR HUMANS TO HOLD ON TO CAUSE THEY'RE SCARED!!

For some reason most dogs prefer to sit in the driver's seat while they are waiting in a vehicle. I used to have a truck with a column shift, or "three on the tree" as it was called, and I worried that the dog would accidentally pull it out of gear while I was gone. Since you can't put details on small figures, it's best to use silhouettes or shades as I have on this page.

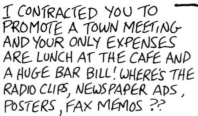

I HATE THIS LOCAL HIRE POLICY!!
95-46

I CONTRACTED YOU TO PROMOTE A TOWN MEETING AND YOUR ONLY EXPENSES ARE LUNCH AT THE CAFE AND A HUGE BAR BILL! WHERE'S THE RADIO CLIPS, NEWSPAPER ADS, POSTERS, FAX MEMOS ??
©D.URQUHART

I MEAN WHAT KIND OF 'COMMUNICATIONS CONSULTANT' ARE YOU??
TOWN HALL
OH! THE BEST!!

Locals know best. In Aklavik, our Porcupine Caribou Management Board was told that our public meeting could never compete with radio bingo that night. So instead, we went down to the local station and had the caller advertise our meeting at the community hall right after bingo ended. We offered free prizes for attendance and got the best public turnout the town had seen in years.

WHAT EXACTLY MAKES YOUR LIFESTYLE SO UNIQUE?
©D.URQUHART
"TWO PATHS DIVERGED IN THE WOODS AND I..."
"I WALKED STRAIGHT INTO THE @★* BUSH BETWEEN THEM..."
"AND THAT HAS MADE ALL THE DIFFERENCE!"
95-47

Robert Frost's poem says "And I, I chose the one less traveled by," in praise of personal courage and individuality. But he still chose an existing path. I prefer the notion of blazing your own trail in life. I've had requests for copies of this strip.

GOODBYE TOURISTS! GOODBYE HUNTERS! GOODBYE SCIENTISTS! GOODBYE STUDENTS! GOODBYE FILM MAKERS! GOODBYE MINERS! GOODBYE JOURNALISTS! GOODBYE ARTISTS! SEE YOU NEXT SUMMER!!
95-48
COME VISIT
THE NORTH
ADVENTURE
SCENERY
DATA
RESOURCES
©D.URQUHART
AND SO BEGINS AN ANOTHER YEAR IN THE TRUE NORTH!

I saw this strip taped to the mirror behind the homeliest, most down to earth bar in Whitehorse. If there is a lot of text in a box, you can omit the speech bubble and just draw a little arc to the speaker.

SKOOKUM'S TRUE NORTH
95-49
AMAZING HOW ALL THESE ASPENS LOOK ALIKE AND TURN THE SAME COLOUR IN FALL!
NOT REALLY! THEY'RE ALL ONE PLANT!
YOU MEAN THEY'RE NOT INDIVIDUALS?
NOPE! ALL ONE ROOT SYSTEM AND GENETICALLY IDENTICAL...
MAKING ASPEN GROVES THE BIGGEST PLANTS IN THE WORLD!
TAKE THAT MR. GUINESS!

Observing aspens changing colour in the fall, my wife and I often remarked how a cluster of trees would turn exactly the same hue, while a nearby group will all become a very different shade. It never occurred to us that all the trees of the same colour were just one plant until we read it in Discover magazine.

ROSIE IS FED UP WITH DRUNKEN HUNTERS...
ANOTHER WHISKEY CAPTAIN MORANGIE?
AND SHE'S GOING TO STAND UP TO HIM LIKE A REAL, NORTHERN WOMAN.
IN THE COLONIES I ALWAYS CARRY SPIRITS IN CASE I SEE A SNAKE!
BUT THERE ARE NO SNAKES IN THE NORTH!
RIGHT! WHICH IS WHY...
I CARRY THIS ONE!
OH WELL! SHE STOOD UP FOR A WHILE!

This is a W.C. Fields quote that I used to portray a problem in outfitter camps where heavy drinking by hunters is quite common. Some hunters require a lot of babying. In a hunting cartoon book I did years ago, I portrayed a hunter who had to be read to every night like a child so he could get to sleep. A friend of mine who is a guide told me he once ripped that page out of the book and stuck it on the outhouse door in order to cure his hunter from endless complaining.

DON'T CHOP THAT!
SEE? HANDLES!
DON'T CUT THAT!
SEE? HANDLES!
WHICH SHOWS THAT BUSH LIFE IS EASY...
95-51

©D. URQUHART
IF YOU KNOW HOW TO HANDLE IT!

I learned the trick of making holes in the hide while hunting with some Dogrib elders from Fort Rae in the Northwest Territories. The log handles are my own invention from years of cabin building. I like to introduce northern realism whenever possible. Notice the tendons dangling from the hoof in Skookum's mouth. If you pull them you can make the whole hoof contract.

1995
GAWD! IT'S LATE FALL AND THERE'S STILL FLIES BUGGING ME!!
I HATE FLIES!
SNAP! SNAP!
SNAP!
SNAP!!
OH! YOU'RE A DEAD MAN! YOU'RE DOG MEAT!
© D. URQUHART
95-52

I bet most families tease their pets in gentle ways. One time in the bush, I put a wolf hide over my head and skulked around the dog yard. It caused quite a sensation!

WHY ARE MEN ALWAYS THROWING ROCKS?
SEVEN! BEAT THAT BOY!
© D. URQUHART

THEY'RE VERY PRIMITIVE! AFTER ALL WHAT IS A BULLET BUT A VERY FAST ROCK?

WHAT'S AN AXE BUT A STICK WITH A SHARP ROCK ON IT?
SO WHY DO WE BOTHER WITH MEN?

THEY KEEP THE CABIN WARM AND MEAT ON THE TABLE!
95-53

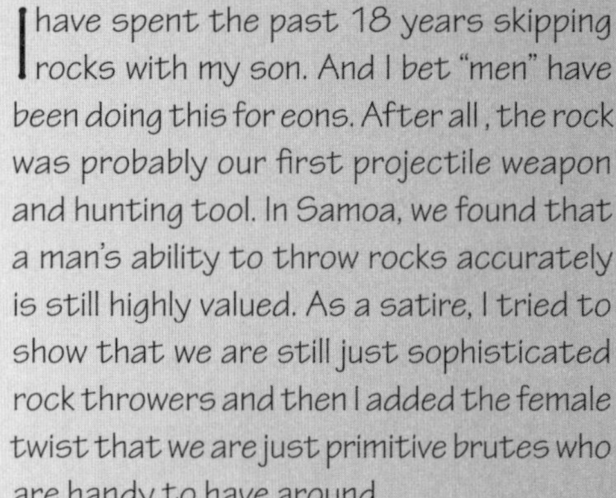

I have spent the past 18 years skipping rocks with my son. And I bet "men" have been doing this for eons. After all, the rock was probably our first projectile weapon and hunting tool. In Samoa, we found that a man's ability to throw rocks accurately is still highly valued. As a satire, I tried to show that we are still just sophisticated rock throwers and then I added the female twist that we are just primitive brutes who are handy to have around.

stephanie
MARTEN'S GOT HIS SPLITTING MAUL STUCK IN A LOG
95-54
WHAM
WHAM!

NOW HE'S BURIED BOTH WEDGES AND HIS PICKAXE...
BOOM!
YOU SPLIT THE WOOD WITH DYNAMITE!!
NORTHERNERS NEVER SAY DIE!!
YOUR KINDLING!

I've done everything but the dynamite and on occasion if it had been handy I might have been tempted. I worked a lot on Marten's expressions to give them the right manic look.

HEY! YOU'RE BACK! WE'RE GOIN' TO THE BAR TONIGHT! WANT TO COME?
UH...UH....

WHAT'S THE MATTER WITH HIM?
95-55
AH...

THREE MONTHS ALONE IN THE BUSH...
OH...OH.
© D. URQUHART

AND HE AIN'T USE TO TALKIN' YET!
OH...OKAY?

This is my university friend Gary again. The strip is based on experiences my wife and I had with loss of language skills in isolation. Recently, I read about hospital studies called the "lazy brain syndrome" which show that people's mental abilities begin to deteriorate after lack of stimulation for as little as 3 weeks.

SIGH! THERE'S MARTEN'S NEW TRAPLINE...

HE'S DOWN THERE CUTTING LINES, HUNTING AND FISHING WHILE I'M OFF TO ANOTHER ✱@✱ BUSINESS MEETING!!
95-56

MEMO: OCTOBER 30 1995...
© D. URQUHART
I HATE MY LIFE!!

When you are going happily about your daily business in the bush, you watch the jets pass high overhead and idly wonder what those people are doing and where they are going. For a moment, it may appear glamorous to be streaking by with your in-flight movie and meal tray. I reversed this perspective to the passengers' viewpoint in order to comment on the sterility of most business lives.

SO? WHAT PART OF THE NORTH ARE YOU FROM?
FORT DOGGEREL! BUT HOW'D YOU KNOW I'M A NORTHERNER?
95-60

WELL, IT'S SIX DEGREES BELOW FREEZING AND..

YOU'RE STILL IN SHORT SLEEVES!
BUS STOP

Just recently, I was in Toronto where it was −10°C and snowy. I wore only a suit outside and people kept asking me where my overcoat was. They were all bundled up like Russians. Most cartoonists draw city backdrops as shaded rectangles like this.

A MOUSE! A MOUSE!
ROSIE GET DOWN!

NORTHERNERS AREN'T AFRAID OF MICE!
THAT WAS BEFORE THEY CARRIED HANTAVIRUS WHICH KILLS 50% OF THE HUMANS IT INFECTS!

SKOOKUM! GET YOUR BUTT IN HERE NOW!
©D. URQUHART
95-61

I know the woman who documented the first appearance of Hantavirus in the Yukon. It caused some public alarm and led to ridiculous radio bulletins like, "Don't sleep under trees where mice have been!" Hantavirus has caused many deaths among the Navajo and Hopi in Arizona and the connection with mice first came from elders' traditional knowledge.

"MY DAD IS VERY CLOSE TO NATURE..."

"EVERY MORNING AFTER COFFEE HE HEARS NATURE CALLING HIM..."

"BUT I'VE NEVER FIGURED OUT WHY HE AND NATURE ALWAYS PLAN TO MEET..."

IN THE OUTHOUSE?
95-62
©D. URQUHART

A combination of two cliches: "Being close to nature" and "Hearing the call of nature."

MOST OF WINCHESTER'S CLASS HAVE BIRTHDAYS IN SEPTEMBER AND OCTOBER! ISN'T THAT AMAZING?!!

NOT REALLY! WHEN YOU REALIZE THAT DECEMBER AND JANUARY ARE...
©D. URQUHART

THE COLDEST AND DARKEST MONTHS!
95-63

I heard this as a joke 30 years ago when I first came to the Northwest Territories. It's a nudge-nudge wink-wink answer to "What do northerners do during the long dark period?"

1995

ROSIE KNOWS I GET BACK FROM THE LINE CABIN TODAY SO SHE'LL HAVE BAKED MY FAVORITE BROWNIES!!
©D. URQUHART
LOOKS LIKE WE GOT VISITORS!
95-64
HEY MARTEN! ROSIE'S BROWNIES ARE GREAT! WE JUST CLEANED HER RIGHT OUT OF THEM!!
SIGH! THE BUSH ETHIC: GUESTS GET THE BEST - AT ANY PRICE!

This happened to us when we lived in the bush. After months without seeing anyone, we got a surprise visit from the conservation officer and his pilot. Judi fed them her new baking and it took us a whole day to calm down after they left.

Identity

1996

I STALK THEM!
I SHOOT THEM!
I EAT THEM!

Being confronted with the harsh realities of life and death in the north, northerners are down-to-earth, practical people who are deliberately unsophisticated and decidedly unimpressed by southern pretensions. In a potentially dangerous natural environment, northerners take pride in their bush sense, always try to keep their word and look out for others. They are thus suspicious of strangers from gentler regions who make dangerous mistakes or do not react quickly to emergencies.

I DON'T GET IT! I DRESS LIKE YOU DO! CUSS LIKE YOU DO! DRIVE A 4x4, CHEW SNOOSE AND DRINK BEER! BUT YOU STILL KNOW I'M A SOUTHERNER!
©D.URQUHART

SUCCESS MEANS NOTHING TO YOU?!
SURE! IT MEANS NOT WORKING HARDER!
©D.URQUHART

1996

JERRY REALLY HATED THE BUSH WHEN HE WAS YOUNGER
©D.URQUHART
96-01

BUT NOW HE'S THIRTEEN HE'S OUT EVERY DAY NO MATTER HOW COLD IT GETS!

I HATE THE ☆6 NORTH!
*☆COLD *!! SNOW 6☆ TREES!
I'M MOVIN' TO MY UNCLE'S IN THE CITY!!

I tried to contrast the fact that kids who hate the out of doors actually spend a great deal of time outside so they can smoke.

HUSKIES ARE BROTHER TO THE WOLF AND COUSINS OF THE FOX!!

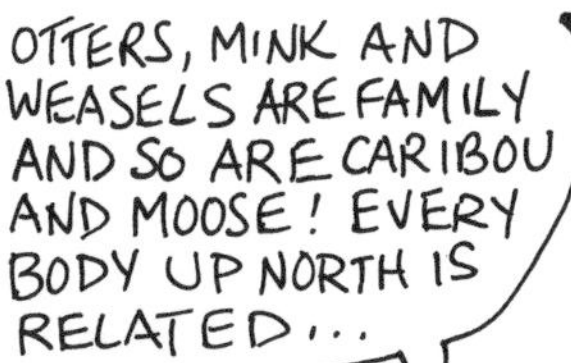

OTTERS, MINK AND WEASELS ARE FAMILY AND SO ARE CARIBOU AND MOOSE! EVERY BODY UP NORTH IS RELATED...

BUT YOU'RE JUST A BIG LONELY MONKEY SO FAR FROM HOME YOU HAVE TO WEAR OTHER ANIMAL'S SKINS TO STAY WARM!
©D.URQUHART

GUESS I SHOULDN'T HAVE CALLED HIM A MONGEREL!
96-02

I wanted to get Skookum higher than Marten by panel three so he could be shouting down at him. I tinkered a lot with how to make this observation about humans being the odd animal in the north. I had all the dialogue ready for Skookum but no reason for him to be shouting at Marten. Then I hit on the insult idea. I am basically a thick and thin pen artist. I used a thick pen in panel 3 for dramatic effect.

CHINK! CHINK!
CHINK!

EARS EVER ALERT TO THE SOUND OF WORK, THE VETERAN HUSKY QUIETLY DEPARTS!

96-03

HUMANS ARE SO DUMB! THEY NEVER NOTICE WHAT'S GOING ON!
©D.URQUHART

GOING SOMEWHERE BOYS??

Our sled dogs were always very alert to our subtlest actions in and around the dog yard. One tiny chink of the harnesses and those who did not want to pull would dive for their houses. I usually portray Marten's dogs as untied because it gives more flexibility to the strip. Many mushers let a dog or two off in sequence to run around and visit the others to relieve the tedium of the dog line.

HERE MARTEN! THIS LADY HAS LESS IN HER CART!!

96-04
GEE ROSIE! FOR A NORTHERNER YOU SURE KNOW CITY WAYS!!

AND HERE'S 8 SALE COUPONS.... AND I WANT 13 LOTTERY TICKETS... PLUS A CARTON OF PLAYERS LIGHTS... AND I NEED A PRICE CHECK ON THESE 3 ITEMS....
© D. URQUHART

This is a simple little joke that happens to everyone but I put it in the context of the northern schizophrenia which is proud of having southern sophistication while disdaining the same society.

WHAT THE HELL IS A VIDEO CAMERA DOING IN A TREE 60 MILES FROM TOWN?!!

96-05
SOME UNIVERSITY KIDS HOOKED IT UP TO THE INTERNET SO PEOPLE CAN SEE THE NORTH!
I'M SO SORRY MARTEN THAT YOUR BUSH HAS BEEN INVADED BY THE WORLD!!
© D. URQUHART
DEU

I DID IT MY WAY
AND THE WEIRDNESS OF NORTHERNERS HAS BEEN CONFIRMED!

This is a true story. Back in 1996, static cams were just gaining popularity. I couldn't believe it when my friend Gary first told me about this university project. Nowadays you can call up any number of them on the Internet.

IMAGINE! THE ANCIENTS BELIEVED THAT STARS WERE FLAWS IN A SHIELD BETWEEN US AND THE GLORY OF THE HEAVENS!

WELL SCIENCE SURE EXPLODED THAT MYTH!!
96-06
© D. URQUHART
DEU

This theory of the universe was popular in Aristotle's time. The Greek philosophers were highly sophisticated thinkers and so enamored with their rational abilities that they expected within a generation to have explained the entire universe and all its workings. Our modern scientists often appear just as smug to me – hence the cartoon.

WITH NEW TECHNOLOGY WE CAN ANALYZE TRACE ELEMENTS IN POLLUTION!

DOES THAT MEAN YOU CAN STOP IT?
HECK NO!

BUT NOW WE KNOW PRECISELY WHERE IT COMES FROM!!
96-07
© D. URQUHART

I've had several requests to reprint this strip which suggests to me that many people are getting fed up with science that leads nowhere. We have desperately serious global environmental problems but there is precious little benefit in endlessly documenting our environmental decline without doing anything about it.

AH! MONSIEUR MARTEN! BACK IN ZEE CITY AGAIN?
YEP! WE'LL HAVE MY USUAL!!

WHAT'S YOUR USUAL?

SMOKED HAM, SMOKED OYSTERS, SMOKED CHEESE, SMOKED SALMON, SMOKED TEA, SMOKED TURKEY...
96-08
© D. URQUHART

Some thirty years ago, I lived in Sachs Harbour on Banks Island where the Inuit trappers loved Lapsang Souchong tea for its smoky taste. When the local trader substituted jasmine tea one year, they were outraged because they had to dump an entire box into one pot in order to get "good colour" and of course by then, it tasted like perfume.

THE GOVERNMENT REGRETS THAT IT MUST SUSPEND THE PARKS PROJECT..
© D. URQUHART

BUT THAT ABROGRATES YOUR FEDUCIARY RES-PONSIBILITY SPECIFIED IN SECTION 16.12.E
96-09
WHO THE HELL IS HE?

YOUR WORST NIGHTMARE!
A NORTHERNER WITH A LAW DEGREE!

Occasionally, people raised in the north survive the entire educational gauntlet and come out with professional degrees. Such people are in extremely high demand because northerners trust them and they understand how to deal with southerners on their own terms.

IT'S SIMPLE! YOUR TOWN MUST REDUCE ITS SOCIAL PROBLEMS, INCREASE JOB SKILLS AND DIVERSIFY YOUR ECONOMY!
SAY! THIS SHOULD INTEREST YOU!
©D. URQUHART

SO? IT'S AN ARMCHAIR!
WHICH IS OBVIOUSLY YOUR ONLY AREA . . .
96-10

OF EXPERTISE!

I get angry even when I reread this cartoon because it represents the endless time and resources wasted by so-called experts who breeze into town, make their superficial assessments of what appear to be simple village economies and then come out with these ridiculous pronouncements. Usually nothing ever changes because the communities have evolved to their present state for a variety of complicated reasons.

SKOOK! YOU CAN'T FIND THE TRAIL UNDER FRESH SNOW??!
GOT TO FEEL IT WITH YOUR FEET! WATCH A REAL EXPERT!!
96-11
10!
7!
8!
CONGRATULATIONS! YOU MADE IT TWO STEPS FARTHER THAN ANYONE BET!
©D. URQUHART

It's a rare lead dog who can feel the hard packed trail beneath a fresh dump of deep snow. And it is a huge annoyance if you are trying to get somewhere and your dogs keep "falling off" the trail.

MARTEN! THANK GOD YOU'RE BACK FROM THE BUSH!!
THE FREEZER'S PACKED IN AT THE RINK!
WE NEED YOUR COMMENTS ON THE TOURISM PROPOSAL!!
THE WHOLE TOWN COUNCIL RESIGNED!
THEY APPROVED THE NEW ROAD!!
WHERE'S THE KEY TO THE REC CENTRE?
96-12

STOP GAZING OUT THE WINDOW AT THE BUSH AND HEAVING BIG SIGHS!!

As a long-time resident of small northern communities, I have often witnessed how such towns rely on relatively few capable and dedicated people. It is called the "20-80 rule" — 20% of the people do 80% of the work. When such people leave town, chaos ensues.

AT LAST! A HOLIDAY OUT OF THE NORTH WHERE WE'RE NOT AT EVERYBODY'S BECK AND CALL!

YO! BRO! YOU SAVVY DAMN TING BOUT DIS MUDDAH?!!

96-13
IT'S ONLY 'TIL SATURDAY WHEN HIS COUSIN GETS BACK FROM THE MAINLAND!
©D. URQUHART

There is a global brotherhood among those who understand heavy equipment. I coupled this idea with the fundamental northern code that you always help people who need it, plus, skilled mechanics are constantly being asked for "help" in small communities.

WOW! LOOK AT THAT FOREST!!
©D. URQUHART

AND THOSE LAKES! AND RIVERS AND OPEN SPACES!!!

FIRST HOLIDAY UP NORTH?
96-14

NO! WE WERE ON HOLIDAYS

AND WE'RE JUST COMING HOME!!

I feel like this every time I come home, and I hear similar sentiments from others returning from winter holidays. It's akin to the wave of peaceful rest that comes over you when you hit the Alaska Highway, driving north from Hudson's Hope!

96-15 ©D. URQUHART
EYAAAH!!
IT'S OKAY MARTEN! YOU WERE HAVING A YUPPIE NIGHTMARE!

One night when we were living in the bush, I had a dream that a gas station had been built in front of our cabin. The dream was so real I got up and checked out the bedroom window. For 25 years I have been plagued by such nightmares but as I learn to recognize them in my sleep, my brain changes some element to fool me yet again. One time I wrote down all the variations that tricked me and that stopped my brain for a while but then it thought up new wrinkles. I need counselling!

IN THE NORTH IT'S SURVIVAL OF THE FITTEST, SKOOK! GOTTA BE ONE STEP AHEAD OF THE COMPETITION WITH MY NEW BOBCAT AND TRAILER I'LL CORNER THE CONSTRUCTION MARKET IN FT. DOGGEREL!!
WAIT 'TIL THE GUYS AT THE CAFE SEE THIS?
© D. URQUHART
96-16
FORT DOGGEREL CAFE

When bobcats first appeared, everyone who ever dreamed about being a small contractor went out and bought one. Overnight the yellow pages were full of bobcat entrepreneurs.

YOU'RE WEARING A SKIRT?!!
YES! SO WHAT?
WELL... THAT IS... UH.... I MEAN...
RECALL! RECALL! RECALL! INPUT: NORTHERN WOMAN WEARING SKIRT IN THE BUSH!! SEARCH UNDER: WOMEN WEIRD BEHAVIOUR, DATES PLACES, OCCASIONS...
IS IT FOR THE ANNIVERSARY OF YOUR FIRST TRIP TO THE TRAPLINE?
96-17
YOU REMEMBERED!!
© D. URQUHART
THE NORTHERN SUPER COMPUTER!

This strip arose from a story I heard about a First Nation lawyer who became famous during the Yukon Land Claims negotiations. He had a phenomenal "computer" memory and used to chant, "Recall! Recall! Recall!" to himself when trying to retrieve an obscure point of law. I coupled this with a bush version of the dichotomy in every marriage about what constitutes a "memorable" occasion.

SO SKOOKUM? WHAT DID YOU DO TODAY?

WELL, I CHEWED AN OLD BEAVER TAIL, ATE A ROTTEN FISH, SUCKED MARROW FROM A PUTRID MOOSE BONE AND DRANK SOME SCUMMY WATER!
© D. URQUHART
96-18

CAN'T YOU TELL FROM MY BREATH??

I have seen a truck of tough northern men emptied by a dog's burp.

SO! OLD JAKE FINALLY SPLIT UP WITH MARTHA!
GOOD THING TOO! HE'S SO IMMATURE!!
© D. URQUHART
NOW HE'S SHACKED UP WITH JENNY!!
WHAT! SHES 20 YEARS YOUNGER!!
96-19

WELL, YOU SAID HE'S IMMATURE!!
THAT'S COMPLETELY DIFFERENT!!
WHICH TAKES THE AVERAGE MALE A LIFETIME TO UNDERSTAND!!

This illustrates my theory that women make all the basic rules for our society and men just try to keep between the lines. I have always tried to describe northern life in a more candid fashion than politically and socially correct southern strips do with their material. Thus, I occasionally use swear words, or terms like "shacked up" which offend a few but are appreciated by the majority.

I JUST BOUGHT THIS AT THE BOREAL MUSEUM AUCTION!
96-20

MY GREAT GREAT GRANDADDY MADE THIS FOR HIS SON'S FIRST HUNT!
© D. URQUHART

NEVER COLLECT ARTIFACTS FROM CULTURES YOU'RE FRIENDLY WITH!!

As a biologist fresh from graduate school, I spent a few weeks with several Inuit families south of Coppermine. One day I returned to camp with some prized "artifacts" including a small mukluk and an antler spoon. My friend gently informed me that the mukluk belonged to his little daughter and had been left behind at their camp the previous year. I was very embarrassed.

ISN'T IT LOVELY TO HEAR THE SWEET BIRD SONGS IN SPRING?
96-21

FLAP YOUR TINY WINGS AND FLY AWAY! PLEASE! FOREVER!
BYE BYE BIRDIE! DON'T CRY BIRDIE! JUST DIE BIRDIE!
THIS LAND IS MY LAND!! THIS LAND'S NOT YOUR LAND!
MY TREE! MY TREE! MY TREE! MY TREE!
SWALLOWS GO BACK TO CAPISTRANO!!
BEAT IT YAHOOS! BEAT IT YAHOOS! IT'S THE WOODY WOODPECKER SONG!
IF A TREE FALLS IN THE FOREST I HOPE YOUR NEST IS IN IT!!
© D. URQUHART

When I was a kid, some recent research on the territorial function of bird songs led to the common understanding that, in spring, birds weren't happily celebrating life but rather shouting nastily at one another. It proved quite a shock to our "Bambi" society and many were angry that dispassionate science had ruined the simple enjoyment of bird songs. Nowadays people seem to accept the scientific version while retaining their romantic appreciation.

ALL READY?
YEP!
OKAY! LET'S GO!!
EVER WONDER WHY THE GROOM ALWAYS WAITS FOR THE BRIDE AT THE ALTAR?
NO?
©D. URQUHART
IT'S FOR PRACTICE!
96-22

Many times I have sat in our truck with my son and said to him. "What are we doing?" to which he cheerfully replies, "Waiting for women!" One night my wife told me a fax joke about how men say, "It's bedtime!" and go straight to bed, while women settle the house for the night and then turn up 20 minutes later. My wife maintains the same thing happens when we leave the house.

WHY IS THAT AREA CIRCLED?
HIGH MOOSE DENSITY
MARK TWAIN SAID THERE ARE THREE KINDS OF LIES...
THERE ARE NO MOOSE THERE!
OH YES! WE HAVE A GIS PROGRAM
LIES, DAMNED LIES AND STATISTICS!
THAT PLOTS THE HARVEST LOCATIONS FROM ALL THE HUNTER REPORT FORMS!
96-23
NOW WE HAVE A FOURTH!
BUT NOBODY REPORTS EXACTLY WHERE THEY ARE SUCCESSFUL!!
G.I.S.*!!
© D. URQUHART
* GEOGRAPHIC INFORMATION SYSTEM

We were watching a GIS demonstration in Mayo by a technician who had plotted all the caribou harvests around the community. It was very impressive to watch the numbers pop up on the map, however, the locals kept saying, "That's not right!" and recounting all the other kills they knew of by hearsay that never got recorded or plotted. For some reason, the power of data increases the more it is analyzed and distanced from its humble origins.

NO! NO! IT'S A MODEL 3CDEE GASKET NOT BC3DE!!
YOU KNOW! IT'S THE BIG ONE WE ALL CALL...
THE DOLLY PARTON!!
96-24
© D. URQUHART

Single-side band radios are notorious for fuzzy transmissions. This is how Alpha, Bravo, Charlie got invented. Satellite phones are rapidly making this strip a history piece. During the Second World War, the bulky life vests were referred to as "Mae Wests."

SEEN THE NEW WAITRESS?
YEAH! HER NAME'S SARA AND IS SHE A KNOCKOUT!

COMES FROM 100 MILE HOUSE WHERE HER DAD'S AN OUTFITTER. GRADUATED FROM COLLEGE IN WILDLIFE MANAGEMENT. JOEY ASKED HER OUT BUT SHE'S GOT HER EYE ON PETE!
96-25

YOU GUYS HEAR ABOUT THE NEW WAITRESS?
UH? NO?

MEN NEVER KNOW WHAT'S GOING ON!
© D. URQUHART

Men are very capable of paying attention when it suits them. And just as capable of playing dumb.

HOW FAR NOW HAL? WE CAN'T TAKE MUCH MORE!!

LOOK! WE'RE SAVED!!!
96-26
© D. URQUHART

THE PAVEMENT HURTS THEIR FEET!!

For more than 14 years I have lobbied the halls of the U.S. Congress to save the calving grounds of the Porcupine Caribou Herd. When I arrived in Washington I was told the first rule of lobbying is, "Wear comfortable shoes." Even so, at the end of a hectic 3 days we northerners were still all limping around.

THE RABID RIVER VALLEY!!
DAMSITE DESTRUCTION!
MUSH LAKE MARSH!
HABITATS AT RISK!
96-27
MOOSE BERRY MOUNTAIN!
UNMITIGATED MINERAL EXTRACTION!!

HAVE A GOOD TRIP?
SUCH POTENTIAL FOR ECOLOGICAL DEGREDATION!!
IMPENDING ENVIRONMENTAL DOOM!!!
IN OTHER WORDS THEY LOVED IT!!

There is a cohort of environmentalists that seems to thrive on doom and gloom. Their rhetoric and writing resemble a doomsday cult. Many of them are fine people but they need to lighten up. This would help gain them more credibility. Moose Berry is a little village near Ft. Doggerel. Moose berries are the hard winter fecal pellets used to make "mosquitoes" and necklaces for tourists.

1996

THIS MEGAPROJECT WILL BRING PROGRESS AND PROSPERITY TO YOUR SORRY LITTLE TOWN!!
96-28
DO YOU WANT TO SPEND THE REST OF YOUR LIVES IN SHABBY LOG CABINS SURROUNDED BY WILDERNESS IN ISOLATION FROM THE OUTSIDE WORLD??
©D. URQUHART
YES!!
OKAY! CALL BRAZIL WE'RE OUTTA HERE!!

When U.S. Congresspeople come to the caribou communities they are often struck by the apparent poverty and puzzled why such people do not embrace the riches that oil development would bring. Living close to the land is rich and rewarding in invisible ways that defy explanation.

OH! ISN'T SHE SWEET!!
96-29
YECHH!!

FLY AWAY HOME YOU DEAR LITTLE LADY!!
GROSS!!

OH WHY! OH WHY WAS I BORN A MALE LADY BUG!!
©D. URQUHART

We treat many animals as little more than cliches. The "industrious ant," the "cunning fox," the "fierce wolf." Can you imagine a "lady eagle," a "buck bunny" and a "miss jackfish"?

WHAT'S THIS FOR?
IT'S THE $25 RALPH OWES YOU!

BERT OWED JAKE $300 AND JAKE OWED REX $ 225 AND $75 TO RALPA SO BERT GAVE THE $300 TO REX AND REX GAVE ME THE $75 SINCE RALPH OWES ME $50 AND THE $25 IS YOURS IF YOU CAN CHANGE A $100...
96-30
©D. URQUHART

I CAN'T BUT I OWE VIC $50 AND JAKE $50 SO YOU COULD GIVE IT TO JAKE EXCEPT HE OWES RALPH $200 SO...
AND THEY SAY NORTHERNERS DON'T UNDERSTAND ECONOMICS!

Twenty years ago, in an Atlin bar, a friend looked at the soft crumpled faded bills on the table and said, "You know, our money never leaves town." Picking one up that had been written on in ballpoint pen he added, "I made this mark at the miner's picnic 15 years ago!"

YOU NORTHERNERS DON'T UNDERSTAND ENVIRONMENTALISM! IT'S REDUCE, REUSE AND RECYCLE!
WE KNOW!
WE REDUCED THE 6 PACK TO EMPTIES!
96-31

WE REUSED THE CANS!
POW!
POW!
POW!

AND NOW WE'RE RECYCLING THE BEER!

Like everyone, I endorse the three Rs but from time to time it's good to poke fun at those who take on holier than thou pretensions.

LEGEND SAYS RAVEN CREATED ALL THE ANIMALS...
YARF
RIGHT!
YARF!
YARF!

SO WHY DID WE CREATE DOGS?
YARF!
IT WAS A MISTAKE!
YARF!
YARF!
96-32

YARF!
YARF!
BUT AT LEAST WE MADE THEM STUPID!!
YARF!
YARF!

A friend recently looked at this strip again after several years and said he never noticed the chain going behind the doghouse before. For me, every raven cartoon is a flight of fancy. Once you introduce ravens there is no telling exactly where the strip will go or how it will end. For some reason many artists draw ravens with light bills like Heckel and Jeckyll. Dark bills are trickier because there is no easy contrast with the body but at least they are ravens!

I DON'T BELIEVE IT! JUST BECAUSE WE CUT DOWN THE TREES! DAMMED THE RIVER, POLLUTED THE WATER AND ARE PLANNING TO ABANDON THE VALLEY...
96-33

YOU'RE DEMANDING THAT WE DO RECLAMATION?!!

© D. URQUHART
IT'S THE NINETIES!

The beaver, Canada's national mammal, clear cuts, pollutes, interferes with watersheds, overharvests and then abandons the area. It is the antithesis of "sustainable development." Yet, at the same time, it creates wetlands which are essential to the health of our environment. With the decline of trapping, beaver activities are causing increasing public concern in the Yukon. I recently did a couple of "beaver" workshops to figure out what to do about these guys.

AHHH!! NOTHING LIKE A DIP ON A HOT DAY! FEELING THE ICE COLD WATER SOAK INTO MY FUR...
96-34
© D. URQUHART

BUT THE BEST IS YET TO COME!
NO SKOOK! GO AWAY! GO ON!!

BAD DOG!! BAD DOG!!

I swear it's true. Every dog we've ever had behaves this way.

WELL MARTEN! YOU'VE DONE IT!!
WHAT? THEY NEVER CHECKED IN?!!
© D. URQUHART
MUSH LAKE LODGE

YOU FIGURED A WAY TO MAKE A LIVING FROM THE BUSH!!
96-35
OKAY! SEND THE FLIGHT WITH MORE BOOZE AND GRUB AND A NEW COOK!!

I'LL CALL MY LAWYER ABOUT THEIR CHEQUE!
SO? HOW DO YOU FEEL?

I'VE GOT AN ULCER! I CAN'T SLEEP! MY FAMILY HATES ME AND I'M $50,000 IN DEBT!!

It's a paradox. You want a job that keeps you in the bush but such jobs are often so frustrating that you are unhappy all the time you are there. I was content to quit field biology because all my bush time was spent worrying about projects and trying to supervise other people.

DOGS HAVE SPECIAL NIGHT VISION WHICH IS WHY OUR EYES SHINE IN THE DARK
REALLY?
96-36

I THOUGHT IT WAS BECAUSE YOUR HEAD IS EMPTY!

OH YEAH? THEN I GUESS THAT EXPLAINS WHY...
© D. URQUHART

YOUR EYES ARE BROWN!!

This is a twist on the old put down, "You must be full of it..." A dog's night vision is superior to ours because they have a greater percentage of rods that respond only to light and not colour. The rods reflect the light off the back of the retina making those spooky shining eyes in the dark.

THEY THINK THEY'RE JUST SO CUTE THEY CAN GET AWAY WITH ANYTHING! AND CHEEKY! THEY PRETEND THEY CAN'T HEAR ME OR THEY REALLY DON'T UNDERSTAND!!
HERE THEY COME! YOU THINK WE'LL OUTSMART THEM THIS TIME??
©D. URQUHART

DOGS?! I THOUGHT YOU WERE TALKING ABOUT YOUR FAMILY!

96-37
WE ARE!!
©D. URQUHART

We had a couple over to dinner recently and all the while I was aware of their slight discomfort whenever we spoke too much to the dog, commented on his behaviour, gave him treats and so on. People without pets must consider the rest of us quite odd and probably pitiable. Just as we feel about them.

WELL WE ALL WENT TO THE CONFERENCE IN RIO..THEN THE WORKSHOP IN FAIRBANKS ...AND TOOK A COURSE IN VANCOUVER.. ..PLUS A SABBATICAL...
GOVERNMENT BUREAUCRACY OF SMALL BUSINESS LOANS AND COUNSELLING

BUT MR. FISHER YOUR NET PRODUCTIVITY IS NEAR ZERO. YOU CAN'T RUN A BUSINESS WHERE YOUR EMPLOYEES ARE RARELY DOING REAL WORK!
WHY NOT?
©D. URQUHART

93-5
YOU DO!

The north is kind of like ancient China where the mandarins are a privileged class compared to the self-employed locals: steady income, perks, lieu time (time off in lieu (place of) getting paid), sick leave, cost of living adjustments, conferences, stress leave, holidays, housing allowance, isolation pay.

I'M A COMPUTER ANALYST BUT I ALWAYS WANTED TO BE A WILDLIFE BIOLOGIST

SO, TELL ME WHAT YOU DO?
WELL, I HAVE AN OFFICE AND A COMPUTER...
"I WORK ON DATA, WRITE REPORTS, GO TO MEETINGS, LEARN NEW SOFTWARE PROGRAMS, ATTEND WORKSHOPS AND CONFERENCES, SUPERVISE STAFF, DO PERFORMANCE APPRAISALS, HEAR UNION GRIEVANCES, APPLY FOR JOB PROMOTIONS, LISTEN TO STRESS RELIEF TAPES, FLIRT WITH SECRETARIES..."
96-39

SOUNDS JUST LIKE MY JOB!!!
©D. URQUHART

This sums up several themes from my own life, plus observations of modern biologists. At community workshops I often hear locals comment that you can't learn about wildlife just by flying over them or sitting at a computer. Times are changing though. The Yukon government is stationing regional biologists in communities and these people work with locals on the land and incorporate local and traditional knowledge, plus science, into their programs.

SKOOKUM! GIVE ME THAT BONE!
NOPE! NOPE! NOPE!

NOW, YOU KNOW CHICKEN BONES ARE BAD FOR YOU! ISN'T THAT RIGHT?!!
Y-YES...
96-40

THERE! AREN'T YOU PROUD OF YOURSELF?
©D.URQUHART
DON'T GO NEAR THE HOUSE BOYS!

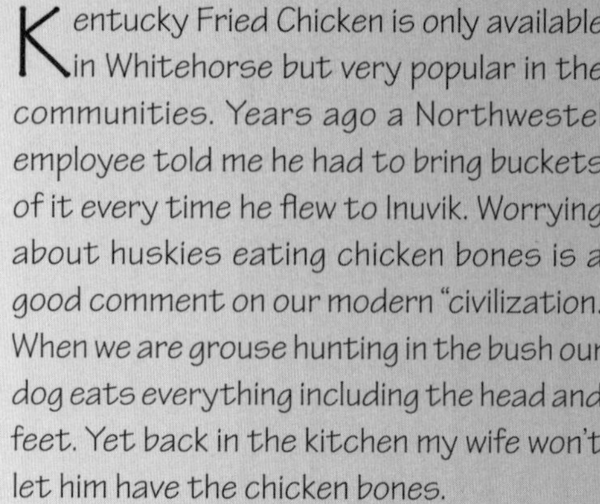
THERE'S A BUNCH OF CRUEL SADISTIC DICTATORS UP THERE!
KFC

Kentucky Fried Chicken is only available in Whitehorse but very popular in the communities. Years ago a Northwestel employee told me he had to bring buckets of it every time he flew to Inuvik. Worrying about huskies eating chicken bones is a good comment on our modern "civilization." When we are grouse hunting in the bush our dog eats everything including the head and feet. Yet back in the kitchen my wife won't let him have the chicken bones.

WELCOME TO THE LAND USE PLANNING WORKSHOP!
MINER'S DON'T KNOW NUTHIN' ABOUT FISH STOCKS!
GOVERNMENT DON'T KNOW NUTHIN' ABOUT CONSERVATION
AND HUMANS DON'T KNOW MUCH ABOUT COOPERATION!
LOGGERS DON'T KNOW NUTHIN' ABOUT TRAPPING!
FARMER'S DON'T KNOW NUTHIN' ABOUT WILDLIFE!
ENVIROMENTALISTS DON'T KNOW NUTHIN' ABOUT BUSINESS!

This came out in the local paper just before a major workshop and people were delighted with it. Actually, workshops are an excellent means of sharing concerns and personal perspectives and I often hear someone say, "Is that all you are worried about?" or "Is that what you thought?" Half of the controversies are resolved in this manner before the core issues even get addressed. Nevertheless, most workshops start out the way I have drawn it here.

SINCE SLY BUCKMASTER WAS INDICTED THE PROGRESS PARTY NEEDS A NEW REPRESENTATIVE!
YEAH! BUT WHO IN DOGGEREL WOULD RUN FOR

THOSE SMASH AND GRAB PROFITEERS!
HEY GUYS GUESS WHAT?!!

THE PROGRESS PARTY HAS ASKED ME TO RUN FOR THEM!!
96-42

BUT VIC! YOU HATE EVERYTHING THEY STAND FOR!!
YOU'RE JUST JEALOUS BECAUSE THEY NEVER ASKED YOU!!
NEVER DISCOUNT THE FLATTERY FACTOR!
CONTINUED

I drew this series during the last Yukon territorial election and, coincidentally, I was writing this commentary on the day the 2000 election was announced.

VIC CONIBEAR IS RUNNING FOR THE PROGRESS PARTY!
IF VIC GETS IN THEY'LL STICK HIM ON THE BACK BENCH FOREVER
VIC'S PRETTY POPULAR BUT HIS PARTY NEVER DID SQUAT FOR DOGGEREL AND THEY HATE NORTHERNERS!
AND HIS PARTY WILL CONTINUE THEIR SMASH AND GRAB POLICIES IN THE NORTH!
96-43
THERE'S ONLY ONE MAN WHO CAN STOP VIC CONIBEAR!
© D. URQUHART
CONTINUED...

MEANWHILE ... BACK AT PROGRESS PARTY HQ...
96-44
WELL VIC, WE'LL TRUST YOU TO PROMOTE OUR PARTY'S PLANS TO SELL OUT TOURISM, OUTFITTING, MINING, OIL AND LOGGING TO FOREIGN INTERESTS!!
ACTUALLY, PEOPLE WANT MORE LOCAL CONTROL OVER SUCH THINGS!
WHICH IS WHY YOU HAVE TO FIND A LOCAL FRONT MAN FOR EACH BUSINESS!
BUT WOULDN'T THAT BE DISHONEST?
WOW! YOU'VE GOT A REAL SENSE OF HUMOUR THERE VIC!
HA! HA! HA! HA! HA! HA! HA!
CONTINUED..

AT THE CANDIDATES DEBATE
AND WHAT ABOUT WILDLIFE HABITAT?
RIGHT! WHO CAN WE SELL IT TO!
MONEY I$ PROGRE$$
NO! NO! I MEAN HOW DO WE DESIGNATE IT FOR PROTECTION!
SIMPLE! AFTER LOGGING, MINING, OIL AND HYDRO DEVELOPMENT...
...WHATEVER IS LEFT BECOMES FULLY PROTECTED!
© D. URQUHART
96-45
YOU SEE VIC... POLITICS ISN'T AS HARD AS IT LOOKS!!
CONTINUED...

After the election was announced, I was discussing the politics of one of our smallest villages, and the subject of why certain people were running for certain parties came up, just like in this strip. Victor Conibear is named after two types of trap. Frank Conibear was a trapper in Ft. Smith, NWT who invented the most popular humane trap in the north. As a game officer, I ran a trap exchange program when I lived in that town.

A few years ago, logging in the Yukon was the big issue and now rumours of a gas pipeline are flying around, so hydrocarbon development will likely form the main economic debate. The primary battle lines are always drawn between business and environmental interests. Caught in the middle are the small communities and especially the First Nations, which have a genuine concern for the land but need to generate revenues just like everybody else.

Recently, I heard this same statement on a national radio satire. In Manitoba, the Protected Areas Strategy provides for an ultimate veto of any proposed protected area by the mining community.

AND NOW OUR NEW NORTHERN CANDIDATE VIC CONIBEAR!!
REMEMBER! STICK TO THE PARTY LINE!!!
© D. URQUHART
FOLKS! BASED ON THE PROGRESS PARTY'S STAND ON ENVIRONMENTAL PROTECTION I URGE YOU...
YOU CAN ALWAYS TELL A NORTHERNER
...TO VOTE FOR MARTEN FISHER!
PROGRE$$
96-46
BUT YOU CAN'T TELL HIM MUCH!!
CONTINUED...

Skookum's comments come from an old Bob Ruzika tune that goes, "Living out in the country a fellow gets a little out of touch. You can always tell a country boy but you can't tell him much." Ruzika was a dentist stationed in Inuvik in the late 1960s. He liked guitar music and played a lot with the locals. It struck him as unfortunate that there wasn't any relevant C&W music. So he decided to write some northern songs. His most famous was "Muktuk Annie."

WELL, THE NORTHERN ALLIANCE GOT IN BY AN UPSET IN DOGGEREL WHICH GIVES MARTEN SOME BARGAINING POWER...
SO HE'S DEMANDING WHAT EVERY BUSHMAN ALWAYS DREAMS OF...
NO BACKBENCH FOR ME GUYS!
MINISTER OF RENEWABLE RESOURCES!!
96-47
© D. URQUHART
YOO HOO! I'M BACK!
CONTINUED.....

Actually this happens quite regularly. I am writing this in Dawson where a former resident who worked on the highways crew became Minister of Renewable Resources. Another Minister was the former chief of the Little Salmon/Carmacks First Nation. Such people have their feet quite firmly planted on the ground but are still bewildered by the bureaucracy when they first get into office.

PATH NARROWS HERE! LADIES FIRST!
THANK YOU! NICE TO SEE YOU'RE STILL A GENTLEMAN IN THE BUSH!!
AGHH!!! GAK!! ECKK!!
96-48
GOOK! UNK! GUGGH! SMACK! SNAP! SLURP!
YOU BUM! YOU JUST WANTED ME TO BREAK TRAIL!!
© D. URQUHART

When my wife leads in the bush she often brandishes a stick to deal with the cobwebs which are surprisingly plentiful.

DAD? WHAT IS THE MEANING OF LIFE? WHAT WAS I PUT HERE TO DO??
COME!
THIS OUGHTA BE GOOD!

©D. URQUHART

96-49

THANKS DAD! I SEE NOW!
THE LESSON THAT CAN'T BE TOLD!

I have seen this strip reprinted several times. In reference to it, one lady told me, "When I take my children into the bush I tell them, 'I am going to show you a secret!'" The profound experience of bush living, coupled with the impossibility of communicating it accurately, is at the core of First Nations traditional knowledge and mystical philosophies like Taoism.

96-50
SO HELMUT AND HANS! DID YOU HAVE A GOOD VACATION IN THE BUSH?!
YA! BUT ZEE NORTH ISS TOUGH PLACE!

DID YOU HAVE SOME BEAR PROBLEMS!!
YA! SURE! YOU TELL US BUY LOTS OF BELLS!
TING! TING!

BUT VEE ABLE TO PUTTING ON
TING! TING!
©D. URQUHART

ONLY THREE BEARS ALL ZUMMER!!
ZEY ARE SILLY DUMPKOFF ANIMALS!

Sometimes, I think if we didn't have European tourists, we'd have to invent them. They provide so many delightful stories. I've never heard of this one, and yet. . . .

MOOSE ARE PERFECTLY ADAPTED TO THE NORTH! I'VE GOT INSULATED HAIR FOR COLD, LONG LEGS FOR SNOW, BIG FEET FOR SWIMMING - EVEN SPECIAL NOSTRILS FOR DIVING!!
96-51
©D. URQUHART

AND WHAT THE HELL HAVE YOU GOT?!
I'VE GOT A GUN!

ASK AN IMPERTINENT QUESTION AND YOU MAY GET A PERTINENT ANSWER!

I began this strip by thinking about how well adapted some animals are to their environment. Whereas, we do not evolve physically but only externally via inventions like cars, planes and guns. Skookum's comment is a quote by a famous mathematician, Jacob Bronowski.

SO! CALF SURVIVAL IS HIGH BUT THE HERD IS DECLINING?
RIGHT!!

THAT MUST MEAN PREDATION IS LOW BUT CALF PRODUCTION IS STILL DOWN!
RIGHT AGAIN!
©D. URQUHART

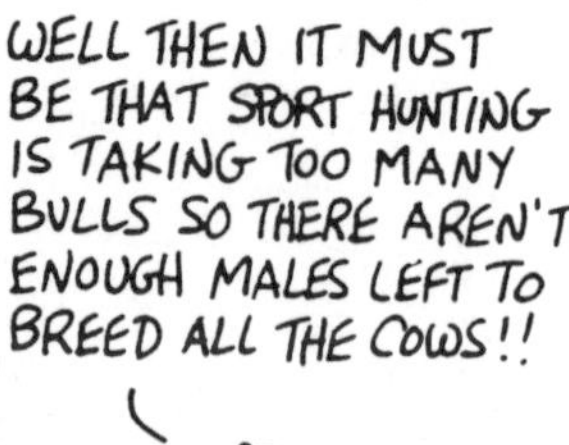
WELL THEN IT MUST BE THAT SPORT HUNTING IS TAKING TOO MANY BULLS SO THERE AREN'T ENOUGH MALES LEFT TO BREED ALL THE COWS!!

96-52

TELL ME ABOUT IT!!

This is a basic tenet of modern wildlife management but the strip outraged the Yukon Outfitter's Association when it appeared in the annual report of the Yukon Fish and Wildlife Management Board.

ROSIE! WE'VE COME TO A **WATERSHED**!!
SIGH! I KNEW THIS WAS COMING!!

WE CAN'T PUT OFF THIS DECISION **ANY LONGER**!!
OKAY! I'M READY TO TAKE THE PLUNGE!!
96-53
© D.R. URQUHART

WE **MUST** TAKE THE NORTH VALLEY TO MUSH LAKE OR THE SOUTH VALLEY TO THE HIGHWAY!!
AND THEY'LL DO IT WITHOUT **PROFESSIONAL COUNSELLING**!

I drew this during a media splurge on marital relations. It struck me that much of the stress that was being discussed resulted from artificial lifestyles. My wife and I never got along so well as we did in the bush. Each of us had a vital role to play and the division of labour and responsibility seemed very natural.

SURE WAS A COLD SUMMER EH? MARTEN?
YEP!

GUESS THE TOURISTS SHOT THROUGH FORT DOGGEREL PRETTY FAST?
I DUNNO! SOME ARE STILL HERE!
FT. DOGGEREL CAMPGROUND
©D. URQUHART 96-54

FROZEN SOLID!!
WE'RE GETTING THE U.S. MILITARY TO AIRLIFT THEM HOME!!

RVers are often alarmed by our northern summers. This strip may become increasingly dated if the present warming trend continues.

MARTEN! LOOK AT THIS GREAT CARIBOU ANTLER!
LEAVE IT! SOME BULL WILL BE LOOKING FOR IT NEXT FALL!
96-55
YOU MEAN THEY HAVE TO FIND THEIR OLD ONES EVERY YEAR?!
SURE! WHY DO YOU THINK..
THEY MIGRATE AROUND ALL THE TIME?!
ULP!! I NEVER THOUGHT ABOUT IT!!
EVERY NORTHERNER IS ALLOWED ONE A YEAR!
ANTLER HERE
©D. URQUHART

This originated as a joke I pulled on a secretary in 1971 while working for the Northwest Territories Game Management Division in Yellowknife. She asked what happened to all the shed caribou antlers and I told her this story. But the James Bay Crees went one better with Samuel Hearne in 1769 when they told him that caribou bulls annually shed their penises and watched him searching all over the tundra for them.

NICE BONE COLLECTION!
©D. URQUHART
MY LIFE'S WORK!!
I'M A BIT OF A COLLECTOR MYSELF!
96-56
REALLY? WHAT DO YOU SPECIALIZE IN?
ROAD KILLS!!
AWESOME!!

On one long trip up the Dempster Highway our dog compiled a bone collection that had to be unloaded from the van every evening so he could admire them and packed up again every morning. It is amazing what some people collect and the north is full of eccentric collectors.

WHAT'S GOING ON HERE?
BLACK TUESDAY! EACH MONTH THE NEW MINISTER MAKES US SHUT DOWN ALL OUR COMPUTERS FOR A WHOLE DAY!!
TOO BAD! I'M DRAFTING HABITAT PROTECTION REGULATIONS FOR THE WILDLIFE ACT!!
HEY! I'M DOING A FULL POLICY REVIEW OF THE SAME THING!!
©D. URQUHART
WE'D BETTER GET TOGETHER ON THIS! HOW'S ABOUT TAKING AN EARLY LUNCH?!
AFTER ALL WE CAN'T GET ANY WORK DONE TODAY!
96-57

"Black Tuesday" is actually the stock market crash of 1982. I saw a blowup of this strip in the cubicle of a policy analyst at the Yukon Department of Renewable Resources. The black shade at the top of panel 3 is a simple way of creating visual emphasis or adding darkness to a light strip.

Tourism

1997

Tourism creates the greatest tension between northerners and southerners, often with hilarious results. It is the ultimate paradox in which northerners share their most prized possessions with people they would be least likely to associate with under normal circumstances. Still, as in all of life, there are lessons to be learned and friendships to be made on both sides.

OKAY! JUST HOLD THAT POT A LITTLE HIGHER!
CLICK
CLICK
CLICK
CLICK

ARE WE READY TO GO TO THE OUTHOUSE?
CAMPGROUND
SIGN IN
©D. URQUHART

97-47
YOU MEAN THERE'S NO SUCH THING AS WILDERNESS?!!
NEVER WAS!!

WASN'T THE FORMER MINISTER COMMITTED TO OPEN GOVERNMENT?
YES HE WAS!
© D. URQUHART

AND TRANSPARENT MANAGEMENT POLICIES?
HIS VERY OWN MOTTO!

THEN WHY ARE YOU SHREDDING ALL HIS DOCUMENTS?!!
HE SAID YOU NORTHERNERS APPRECIATED FIRE STARTER!
97-1

I drew this after the Yukon election when there was a lot of shredding going on during transition to a new government. It's just a satire on political hypocrisy with a northern twist, but what else struck me is the self-inflated importance governments take on. I mean, what dangerous secrets could there really be in this little tin pot territory?

DISCOVERY OF LIFE ON MARS WILL SHAKE YOUR SOCIETY TO ITS VERY ROOTS!

NOPE!
© D. URQUHART

AFTER GALILEO AND DARWIN THERE WAS DRAMATIC RELIGIOUS AND PHILOSOPHICAL UPHEAVAL!!
YEP!
SO WHAT WILL HAPPEN THIS TIME
CARL SAGAN WILL WRITE ANOTHER BOOK AND SELL IT TO HOLLYWOOD, X-FILES WILL HAVE A 2-HOUR SPECIAL, THE TOY, T-SHIRT AND GREETING CARD INDUSTRIES WILL FLOURISH AND THE INQUIRER WILL CLAIM MADONNA AND DENNIS RODMAN REGULARLY MATE WITH MARTIANS!
97-2
SO! AFTER THE AGE OF REASON COMES THE AGE OF TRIVIA?
YEP!

This strip was occasioned by the discovery of a meteorite with apparent signs of life embedded in it. Subsequent controversy has largely dismissed this. What impressed me, however, was the shallow initial response from the public and the media. Nothing is profound anymore; nothing challenges our fundamental beliefs because we have none. Oscar Levant said, "Strip the phony tinsel off Hollywood and you'll find the real tinsel underneath." It's all Hollywood these days.

I'VE GOT A 486 AT HOME BUT ITS NOT POWERFUL ENOUGH!!
REALLY?!! I HAD A .357 MAGNUM BUT IT WAS TOO MUCH!!

WELL, I'M GETTING A 586 THAT ONLY WEIGHS 4.2 POUNDS!
I'LL STICK WITH MY .308 AND ANYTHING UNDER 7 POUNDS IS TOTALLY INACCURATE!
© D. URQUHART

THIS GUY SURE DOESN'T KNOW COMPUTERS!!
THIS DUDE SURE DOESN'T KNOW GUNS!!
97-3

In a parliamentary debate, Benjamin Disraeli accused an opponent of, "using numbers as if they were adjectives!" Today, numbers really are adjectives and have become a modern obsession. Everything has a number, from cars to computers. Computers and guns make a great parody of this because they are both rated on power and weight as well as representing lifestyle extremes.

THEY'VE DISCOVERED LIFE ON MARS!!
WE KNOW!
©D.URQUHART

YOU KNEW BUT YOU NEVER TOLD ANYONE?!
HEY! IT'S TOUGH ENOUGH CONVINCING EVERYBODY WE CREATED THE LAND THE SKY, THE WATER AND ALL THE ANIMALS HERE!! AIN'T NOBODY GONNA BELIEVE

97-4
...WHAT WE DID ON MARS!!

In James Houston's classic, "White Dawn," the Inuit shaman regularly flies to the moon and then reports back to the people who are impressed but totally credulous. Their society had only one story and it all fit together. The advent of modern science split our relationship with the universe into the "science" of the cosmos, which we are compelled to "believe," and the science fiction of Star Trek, which many desperately wish were true.

HOW CAN THOSE CHICKADEES SURVIVE AT 50 BELOW!??
YEAH! IT LOOKS LIKE IF YOU TOUCHED THEM THEY'D JUST...

CRICK!
TINK!
CRICK!
CRICK!
CRICK!!

SHATTER!!
SORRY!!
SORRY!!
SORRY!!
97-5
©D.URQUHART
POP!

How do they survive? With the total volume of a ping pong ball, how does that little heart stay 60 degrees warmer than the temperature half an inch away? I bet, like the aerodynamics of bumblebee flight, that if science were to thoroughly investigate this, it would declare the chickadee a physical impossibility.

MARTEN, WHY DO PEOPLE GET SO SHORT-TEMPERED DURING THE DARK PERIOD?
BECAUSE THEY CAN'T ENJOY SIMPLE PLEASURES LIKE WE DO!

LIKE WATCHING THE EVENING STAR RISE?
RIGHT!

WHACK!!!
ROSIE! WHAT WAS THAT FOR!
YOU WERE BLOCKING MY VIEW! STUPID!!!
97-6

Even with electricity, daily life above the Arctic Circle during the 24-hour dark period is a surreal experience. You work all day in an office where the windows are pitch black, as if you were putting in a late night. At noon, if you go outside, you feel like you should be going home. People tend to become housebound, lethargic and cranky. Many marriages have floundered in the dark period – especially if one partner does not have a job.

1997

8000088!!
KINDA GIVES NEW MEANING...
HUMP
TO THE WORD TAILSPIN, EH?!!
I'M GONNA PUKE!!!
97-7

97-8
NOW YOU'VE DONE IT!!

WELL PROFESSOR! AFTER 20 YEARS UP HERE YOU MUST KNOW A LOT ABOUT NORTHERNERS!
YA! AFTER ONE YEAR I WROTE A WHOLE BOOK!

BUT AFTER 10 YEARS I FELT I KNEW ONLY ENOUGH TO PUBLISH A FEW ARTICLES!

THEN BY 15 YEARS I WAS ONLY CONFIDENT ENOUGH TO MAKE RELIABLE NOTES!!
97-9

AND IF I STICK AROUND MUCH MORE I WON'T KNOW A DAMN THING!!!
A TRUE EXPERT IS BORN!

We had a husky named "Willy" who was normally very brave and aggressive, except when crossing clear ice – even if the water beneath was only a couple of inches deep. He would crawl along on his belly whimpering and gouging the ice with his toenails for a grip. With other dogs we could put on our skates and ride astride them like miniature racehorses which was quite a thrill at full gallop.

There is a northern superstition that if you whistle at the northern lights they will come nearer. Northern lights have always inspired people but recently, they have become a booming tourist attraction. At a hotel in Fairbanks, I saw dozens of Asian couples in identical arctic expedition suits. Someone told me that they believe it is very lucky to conceive a child during the aurora. At Chena Hotsprings, special glass-domed units have been constructed for just that purpose.

This is based on a caution I was given when I first arrived in Yellowknife "brighty-eyed and bushy-tailed," 30 years ago. And, truly, after a few months in the north you have learned so much that you do feel like an expert. The story I was told goes, "After a month in the north you want to write a book. After a few years you want to write an article. After many years you begin to humbly take notes."

AGHH! I HATE THIS CRUD! A HUSKY NEEDS RED MEAT LIKE A WOLF!

OH YEAH? HOW'D YOU LIKE A KICK IN THE HEAD OR GUT EVERY TIME YOU BROUGHT A MOOSE DOWN?
W-W-WO-WOLF?
©.D.URQUHART
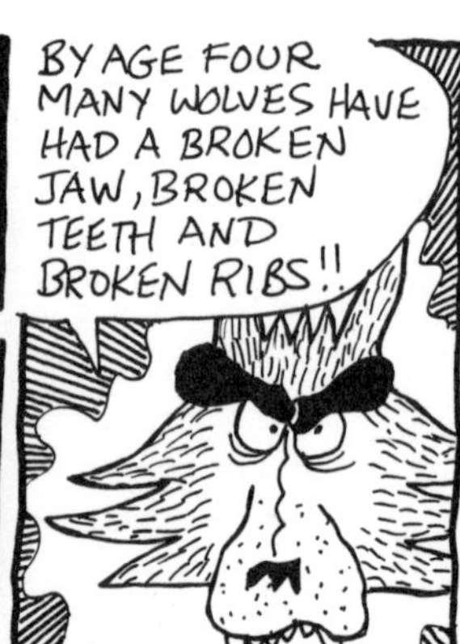
BY AGE FOUR MANY WOLVES HAVE HAD A BROKEN JAW, BROKEN TEETH AND BROKEN RIBS!!

WELL, WELL, IF IT ISN'T OLIVER TWIST! I THOUGHT YOU HATED THIS STUFF!
SHUT UP AND GIVE ME MORE!
97-10

I drew this after talking with a Yukon wolf biologist, so the third panel is true and a sobering comment on the tough life of that species. He also told me that, for a few weeks each spring, several packs will amalgamate and basically "party." In such numbers they can run down anything they want. Occasionally, you hear stories about giant wolf packs and in the 1950s, this, plus a fear of caribou declines, lead to a large-scale poisoning program across the north.

SINCE YOU'RE A NORTHERNER THERE'S A SPECIAL TEST ON YOUR JOB APPLICATION!!

READY? NOW IMAGINE YOU'RE AT THIS DESK...
97-11

...AND IT'S SPRING, THE GEESE HAVE RETURNED, FISH ARE COMING UP THE RIVER, FLOWERS ARE BLOOMING, SOON THERE'LL BE BERRIES TO PICK...

NICE PEOPLE! BUT TRAGICALLY FLAWED!!

Years ago there was a job notice pinned up in the Atlin post office for 3 months steady work as a cook. The notice stayed on the bulletin board for several months because as one lady put it, "No one feels they can commit themselves for that length of time." Not that there were many jobs around, just that to northerners, time and independence are paramount and a "steady job" is often viewed as a sentence.

10,000 YEARS OF EVOLUTION WITH HUMANS HAS CHANGED THE WILD

WOLF TO THE WILEY HUSKY WHO IS A MASTER OF
OH FOR GOD'S SAKE!!

..THE FINE ART OF...
97-12
GIVE HIM SOME!!
©D.URQUHART

BEGGING!!!

I'll bet the "camp dog" was our first domesticated animal. Lap dogs are not convincing proof, but watch huskies when you are camping — prowling around at the edge of the fire light, lying with their backs to the blaze and staring intently into the darkness, barking at strange noises in the bush, and then cadging for meat scraps or a tummy rub. It must have been so comforting to have this wonderful partnership under conditions of constant danger.

WE'RE GEOLOGISTS FROM MAGMACORP! THEY SAY YOU HAVE THE BEST ROCK COLLECTION IN TOWN!
COME IN!
97-13

...AND THIS ONE LOOKS JUST LIKE AUSTRALIA AND HERE'S ONE WITH A KEYHOLE RIGHT THROUGH IT! AND,...

MARTEN! WHY DIDN'T YOU SHOW THEM YOUR MINERAL SAMPLES?
SURE! SO THEY COULD SCOOP ALL MY PROSPECTS! I'M NOT THAT DUMB!!

WHAT A FLAKE! ALL HE COLLECTS IS 'BEAUTY ROCKS'!
©D.URQUHART
YEAH! BUT THREE OF THEM WERE FROM DIAMOND PIPES!!
CONTINUED...

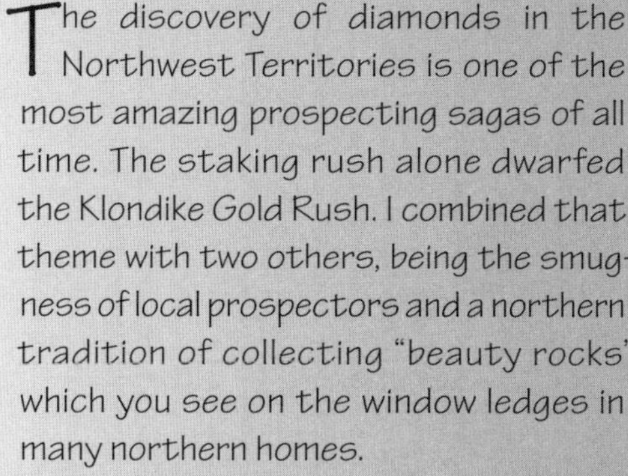

The discovery of diamonds in the Northwest Territories is one of the most amazing prospecting sagas of all time. The staking rush alone dwarfed the Klondike Gold Rush. I combined that theme with two others, being the smugness of local prospectors and a northern tradition of collecting "beauty rocks" which you see on the window ledges in many northern homes.

SOMETHING FUNNY GOING ON! THOSE MAGMA CORP BOYS ARE USING CODE!!
Roger! That's more LUCY at 260' in core DX-120B!

LUCY? LUCIFER? SULPHUR? PHOSPHOROUS? WHAT THE HECK IS LUCY ANYWAY?
LUCY IN THE SKY WITH DIAMONDS!
©D.URQUHART
97-14

DIAMONDS? HAR! HAR! HAR! EVERY PROSPECTOR KNOWS THERE'S NO DIAMONDS IN THE NORTH!!!
AND THEY LAUGHED AT COLUMBUS!

When I was prospecting in northern Quebec we could often hear other prospectors talking in code about their finds on the single side-band radio. When I drew this I was planning to do a long series on the diamond theme. I still have some of the strips in my dresser but for some reason I never used them.

YOU'RE PUTTING OUT PUSSY WILLOWS TOO EARLY!!
97-15
EVOLUTION FAVOURS RISK TAKERS!

WE NEED MUTATIONS FOR SURVIVAL!
OH MARTEN! PUSSY WILLOWS! ALREADY!!

OKAY NOW! HOW'S ABOUT A MUTATION TO SURVIVE IN A GLASS VASE ON A WINDOW SILL!!!

Sometime in February my wife begins her annual pussy willow hunt. And sure enough there is always a bush somewhere that is weeks ahead of the others. From Darwin we learned that selective pressures imposed on natural variation is what drives the evolution of species. The early budding of willows, however, strikes me as an evolutionary dead end thanks to people like my wife.

SORRY I'M LATE! CONFERENCE CALL!
97-16
BULL! YOU TOOK YOUR SECRETARY TO McDONALDS FOR LUNCH!!
I...AH!!... HOW DID YOU KNOW?
FRESH SNOW! TRACKS FROM HER OFFICE DOOR TO YOUR CAR! TRACKS FROM YOUR CAR TO THE DUMPSTER WHERE RAVENS ARE PULLING OUT HAMBURGER CARTONS

I'M SORRY!! SO SORRY!! AND I'LL BRING BACK THE LAPTOP AND THE CAMERA AND PAY FOR MY BOGUS EXPENSE CLAIMS AND THE FIRST CLASS SEATS TO THE CONFERENCE!
© D.R. URQUHART

AS MINISTER YOU GOTTA UNDERSTAND BUREAUCRATS! FIRST YOU GOT POLICY WONKS WHO DON'T CARE WHAT GETS DONE SO LONG AS IT SOUNDS FANCY!

THERE'S PROCESS WONKS WHO DON'T CARE WHAT GETS DONE SO LONG AS ITS CODED RIGHT!

TECHNO WONKS DON'T CARE WHAT GETS DONE SO LONG AS IT NEEDS HIGH TECH EQUIPMENT! AND LOTS OF LESSER WONKS!!
97-17

?
WONK!
WONK!
WONK!
WONK!

ALL RIGHT! MY SOCKET SET!!

MY PRUNING SHEARS!!

MY FRISBEE!

SPRING THAW!

97-18
© D.R. URQUHART
WHEN WINTER GIVES UP HER TREASURES!!
MY FIRST ROADKILL!!
MY MOOSE HIDE!!

It had just finished snowing when we left a Porcupine Caribou Board meeting late one afternoon in Dawson City. Someone asked if "Jack" had already gone to his hotel room and a trapper with us said, "Let's track him out!" Sure enough, in the fresh snow were his prints across the parking lot heading to town. Now how many city folks would have thought of that? I combined this with the theme of "white collar" pilfering and other mischief that happens in all bureaucracies.

As a long time consultant to governments, I have studied the stratification of bureaucracies, beginning with the field staff and working up through increasingly rarefied layers to the policy makers who are often completely out of touch with what is going on. In any major deliberations of the Yukon Fish and Wildlife Management Board, I always ask for the presence of conservation officers to ensure that we do not get carried away with fanciful law making.

This is the kind of strip that, if you don't live in the north you'd say, "Yeah? So what?" But bush types are always busy outside in the winter, bucking up firewood or working on their truck or snowmobile or sleds. Inevitably, tools get forgotten, then buried under new snow. I lost one great little Norlund axe for two years that way.

GOTTA MEND THAT FISH NET!
NEED TO BUY NEW BOOTS!
GOTTA FIX THIS KICKER!
GOTTA FIX THE FLOAT DOCK!!
GOTTA THE
YIKES! GOTTA PATCH THE BOAT
GOTTA BUY A NEW COOLER!!
CHANNEL SURFING THE NORTHERN MIND IN SPRING!
GOTTA MEND THE MOSQUITO NET!!
97-19

Every northerner survives with a collection of gear that is in various states of disrepair. Sometimes you go to repair something and find you have to repair several other things in order to get to that first repair.

YOU COULD BE SECRETARY FOR THE COUNCIL?
I HATE THE MAYOR!

97-20
HOW ABOUT WAITRESSING AT THE CAFÉ?
MEL AND I DON'T GET ALONG!

CAMP COOK AT NEW GOLD?
THE DRILL PUSH IS A PIG!!!

BIG FIRE OUT AT JACKFISH LAKE LAST FALL...
OKAY! OKAY! I'LL PICK MUSHROOMS AGAIN!!
©D.R. URQUHART

Huge forest fires over the past several years in the Yukon have attracted throngs of mushroom pickers from everywhere. And if you think northerners are eccentric!!! Anyway, it definitely appeals to the highly independent character since you are totally your own boss. I combined this theme with the perennial small town problem that everyone knows everyone else a bit too well.

FIRST DAY ON THE JOB AND YOU'RE NOT SURE WHAT TO DO FIRST!!
YOU GOT IT!!

I'LL TELL YA WHAT ALL THE OTHERS DID!!

GRAB SOME PAPERS AND A CUP OF COFFEE AND RUSH ABOUT LOOKING FIERCE!!

97-21
WATCH OUT! THAT NEW MINISTER IS GOING TO KICK SERIOUS BUTT AROUND HERE!!
©D.R. URQUHART

This is a common office joke and this strip is a continuing story about Marten as the Minister of Renewable Resources since he won the election back in strip 96-47. A sub-theme in several strips is his rapport with the cleaning lady, her being the lowest status in the building and him the highest status. But the two are united because they are common folk.

WELL BRIEFLY MR. MINISTER OUR QUANTITATIVE ANALYSIS...
TWEET!!!
UH!...WHY DID YOU DO THAT?
I'M GOING TO BLOW THIS EVERY TIME THERE'S A WORD I DON'T KNOW!!
SHOWS MORTALITY... UH... FACTORS... UH...NEGATIVELY... CORRELATED WITH PREDATION... PARAMETERS... AND REPRODUCTIVE...
TWEET! TWEET! TWEET! TWEET! TWEET!
©D.R.URQUHART
97-22
OKAY!! BOTTOM LINE IS IF WE DON'T STOP HUNTING THIS HERD IS IN THE @☆* TOILET!!
THANK YOU!

This is based on a true story a biologist friend told me about an incident in Alberta. Actually, it involved a planning session with a group of locals who were fed up with scientific jargon. I framed this one and it hangs in his office in Whitehorse.

©D.R.URQUHART

MARTEN!!
97-23

BUT HE LIKES...

GUMMY BEARS!!

Take one husky with a sweet tooth. Open his mouth and impale a gummy bear on each of his lower canines. Sit back and enjoy. (Until your wife comes in and says, "Oh! The poor dog! Why do you do that to him?")

WHAT'S THE MATTER!
THESE PRINTERS ARE VERY TEMPERMENTAL! YOU GIVE THEM EVERYTHING THEY NEED BUT THEY WON'T PRINT!!
WHRRR CLICK! CLICK! CLICK!
PRINT YOU ☆@*!! OR I'LL CUT OUT YOUR BUBBLE JET AND FEED IT TO THE SLED DOGS!!
97-24
SALLY? PLEASE ORDER A DOZEN SWISS ARMY KNIVES AND FORT DOGGEREL BALL CAPS FOR THE STATISTICS DIVISION!!
WHRRR-MMM-MMM-MMM-MMM-MMM-

A commentary on the progressive loss of self-reliance in our modern society. When my wife and I lived in the bush we had only sled dogs and no power tools. There was nothing we couldn't fix on the spot. I read somewhere recently that, in the future, technologists will rule the world because they'll be the only ones who understand how it works.

97-25
DOGS ARE SO DUMB!!

LOOK AT THE TROUBLE YOU'RE HAVING WITH THAT DISH!!

©D.R.URQUHART
YOU'RE RIGHT!!

DISHES ARE A STUPID HUMAN INVENTION!!

I drew this after watching our husky lick a dish across a polished floor, under a table and finally wedge it in a corner of the kitchen behind the garbage can. When we had dog teams, some of the dogs would always dump their dishes before eating.

..AND THESE CITY FOLKS HAD A SPECIAL ROOM WITH A BIG WHITE DOG BOWL IN IT!!

SO I STARTED TO DRINK OUT OF IT BUT THIS LADY CAME IN AND SHOOED ME AWAY!!

97-26
THEN YOU KNOW WHAT SHE DID...

©D.R.URQUHART
SOUTHERNERS ARE SO PRIMITIVE!!

We accept the toilet which, incidentally, was invented by Thomas Crapper. But have you ever seen people's reaction to a bidet when they first encounter one? Similarly, after living in the bush for some length, the idea of keeping a large bowl of standing water in your house for you-know-what becomes increasingly bizarre. But worse is coming to town and finding yourself absentmindedly unzipping your fly in public!

97-27
DID YOU KNOW CARIBOU AND MOOSE HAVE FOUR STOMACHS AND SO DO HUMANS??
NOT HUMANS?!

©D.R.URQUHART

YOU MAY BE RIGHT!!

Lichens, twigs and other moose and caribou food are so coarse and dry that the animals need to chew the material, regurgitate it (the cud), chew it again, bathe it in acids and squeeze it out, reconstitute it again and finally produce those hard moose and caribou pellets that last forever in the bush because there is nothing left for other animals to exploit. A favourite part of the caribou stomach is called "The Bible" because of its page-like folds where fluids are reabsorbed.

1997

WELCOME TO
FT. DOGGEREL
WE'RE NOT ON THE INTERNET
SEE? I TOLD YOU IT'S UNIQUE!!
97-28
©D.R.URQUHART

Heh! Heh! VIC'S FISHIN' TOO SHALLOW! HE'LL NEVER GET NUTHIN'!!

Heh! Heh! MARTEN'S FISHIN' TOO DEEP! HE'LL NEVER CATCH NUTHIN'!!

97-29
©D. URQUHART

I JUST GOTTA ASK... WITH ALL THE PONDS IN THE NORTH...
97-30

WHY DID YOU PICK ONE BESIDE THE BUSIEST HIGHWAY WE HAVE?

YOU'RE RIGHT! THEY'RE FROM THE CITY!!
©D.URQUHART

Boy was this prophetic! In the past three years since I drew this, the Internet has exploded. I know one woman in town who has two personal websites.

Of course they don't have a fish finder. Today's anglers are so efficient that many Yukon lakes are losing their trout populations. The standard solution of Catch and Release fishing is difficult to enforce and besides, some people believe this dishonours an animal that has given itself to you. In a recent Yukon workshop it was acknowledged that this viewpoint is valid but that Catch and Release is essential for management and anglers often consider it as showing respect.

Habituation is a remarkable adaptation of wildlife. I once watched a family of mink playing by the edge of a lake near Yellowknife as a jet fighter escorting a 737 both took off directly overhead. Today, I read that wolves are making a worldwide comeback due to their ability to adapt to human proximity (as long as people don't shoot them).

1997

SKOOKUM'S PRIMER OF THE NORTH
THE NORTHERN LAKE
SEE THE SOUTHERNER. HE IS VERY HOT.
©D. URQUHART

SEE HIM RUN TO THE LAKE.
97-31

SEE HIM DIVE FROM THE DOCK.

SEE HIM FREEZE HIS LITTLE BUTT OFF.
DRU

GREAT RV GRAMPS! FETCH ME ANOTHER FROSTY ONE!!

OKAY YOU ★©✱!!! MAKE MY DAY!!
OFF!
97-32

I SAID STOP!! GODDAMMIT!!
© D. URQUHART
DRU

FLAG LADY FANTASIES!!

MARTEN! WHAT ARE YOU DRINKING!!
JUST LAKE WATER! ITS COLD, CLEAR FRESH AND PURE!!
97-33
GLURG! GLUG! GLUP! GLUP! SPLURK!! SPLUT!!
WHOA! HAL! TAKE IT EASY!

HE WAS RAISED ON THE BOTTLE!!
©D. URQUHART

Southerners fall prey to this northern phenomenon all the time. The day is hot (by our standards), the sun is bright and the lake should be warm, right? Wrong! Around here most lakes are fed by glacier melt, ice-cold underground streams or bog drainage which trickles over permafrost.

In Australia they call them "Lollipop Girls" but no matter where, their life strikes me as a dreadful combination of tedium and frustration. They are usually quite friendly though, which must mean you just have to have the temperament for it. I drew the hunch-backed old man in panel 1 after Gary Larsen's style.

This was the common attitude to northern fresh water when I was a young prospector and we thought nothing of drinking out of the dingiest bogs with tea-coloured water. This is still true with one unfortunate qualifier. The arrival of Giardia, an intestinal parasite courtesy of the beaver, has made people a lot more cautious than they used to be.

AM I SEEING THINGS OR ARE THOSE TWO BABES
...FLAGGING US DOWN!!
THANKS SO MUCH!! CHIVALRY CERTAINLY ISN'T DEAD IN THE NORTH!!
SHUCKS! ITS SORT OF OUR CODE YOU KNOW!
WE WERE JUST GOING TO HAVE A PICNIC! CARE TO JOIN US?!!
97-34
WHAT TOOK YOU SO LONG!!
HEY! ITS THE NORTH! SOMEONE BREAKS DOWN! YOU GOTTA HELP THEM!!

A woman wrote me about her sister and a friend who drove the Alaska Highway one July. When they came to a sign that said, "Chains must be installed," they returned to the nearest town, bought chains, went back to the sign and flagged down a local person to put them on for them. They then drove several hundred miles to the next town with their chains on. But stranger still is that the local never made a comment — just put the chains on, got back in his truck and drove off.

MEL! OUR MARRIAGE IS GOING DOWNHILL!!
8%
© D. URQUHART
97-35
YEAH! IT'S BEEN ROCKY LATELY
HARD TO FOCUS ON OUR PROBLEMS AND GET THE WHOLE PICTURE!
MEL! WE NEED A DIVORCE!!
CHAINS MAY BE REMOVED

I bet some pretty dramatic stuff goes on in those RVs with newly retired couples who have never spent a great deal of time with each other and never before driven through hundreds of miles of "empty" country without any of the regular amusements to distract them from each other.

THIS IS A GREAT TOUR BUSINESS! YOU SHOULD EXPAND IT!!
BUT THEN I'D BE WORKING HARDER!!!
YOU COULD BE RICH, FAMOUS AND POWERFUL!
BUT I'D STILL BE WORKING HARDER!!
SUCCESS MEANS NOTHING TO YOU?!
SURE! IT MEANS NOT WORKING HARDER!
©D. URQUHART
YOU NORTHERNERS ARE VERY TROUBLED PEOPLE!!
SO HOW COME YOU'RE THE ONLY PSYCHIATRIST I'VE EVER MET?
97-36

Time, as northerners know, is the ultimate luxury. In Europe they are introducing a 9-hour-day, four-day work week so that people have less money but more time for personal pursuits and family. North Americans want no part of it. They want their stuff! But northerners are like the famous author Henry David Thoreau of whom Emerson said, "It would cost him less time to supply his wants than another. He was, therefore, secure of his leisure."

IT'S MID JUNE AND IT'S ONLY 10 DEGREES ABOVE FREEZING!!
HEY! IF YOU CAN'T STAND THE COLD...
GET OUT OF THE FREEZER!
97-37
OOoo MARTEN! WAS THAT AN ORIGINAL?!
SHOULD I BE WRITING THESE DOWN?
HARRY TRUMAN ROLL OVER IN YOUR GRAVE!

This is a common situation but a pretty lame joke. So, I thought, "What the heck, I'll present it as a lame joke!" The original saying about heat and the kitchen was on a little plaque on Harry Truman's desk in the oval office. He always credited it to one of his staff. Even that saying has more relevance up north since it obviously came from the era of wood stoves.

SKOOKUM'S
FIELD GUIDE TO SCIENTISTS OF THE NORTH
©D. URQUHART
LIMNOLOGIST
SEISMOLOGIST
BIOLOGIST
PALEOBOTANIST
97-38
PATHOLOGIST

Part of being a tiny total society is that we northerners constantly encounter all strata from dignitaries to politicians to performers to scientists. In bigger populations, the average person rarely encounters such people face to face. Here, every community has its graduate student plus government biologists, foresters, and the summer researchers from universities. The esoteric projects, and even the professional titles these people bear, can be bewildering. Hence the strip.

THE HIGHWAY LODGE HAS CHANGED HANDS AGAIN!
I HOPE THEY'RE MORE TOGETHER THAN THE LAST OWNERS!
SO? YOU'RE NOT TOO LONELY OUT HERE?
GOODNESS NO! THE FOREST CREATURES COMMUNICATE WITH US!!!
EVEN THE TREES TALK TO LESTER!!
THAT'S WHY WE CALL IT WHISPERING PINES!!
97-39
DID THE COFFEE TASTE OKAY TO YOU?
SOMEONE BETTER CALL THEIR RELATIVES REAL SOON!
OO-OO-O

For several years I hustled cartoon books to tourist lodges up and down the Alaska Highway. Some owners were very intense, as if they were escaping something – like the evils of modern society. But operating a highway lodge on a lonely stretch of road is no way to do that and, if they were a little light in the loafers when they arrived, the isolation and pressures of the tourist trade only made them worse.

GAWD! THEIR BEAR BELLS ARE DRIVING ME NUTS!!
TINK! TINK! TINK!
TINK! TINK!
UH-OH! BEAR DUNG! BUT NOT GRIZZLY!
VYE NOT?

BECAUSE IT AIN'T GOT BEAR BELLS IN IT!!
97-40

SIGH! I STILL HEAR 'EM SO I GUESS THAT ONE DIDN'T WORK
TINK!
TINK!
TINK!
TINK.

This is an adaptation of the following joke that was going around Whitehorse. "How do you tell black bear poop from grizzly bear poop? Grizzly poop has the bear bells in it."

WHOA! MARTEN!! STOP AND SMELL THE ROSES!!

THAT'S NOT A ROSE!!
NO! IT'S A METAPHOR!!
97-41
©D. URQUHART

DON'T USE THAT LATIN CRAP!! IT'S JUST AN AVENS!!
I'M TALKING ABOUT LIFE! YOU MORON!!

WHAT DO YOU KNOW ABOUT LIFE?! RUSHING AROUND SO MUCH YOU CAN'T EVEN NAME SIMPLE FLOWERS!
I'LL TEACH HIM ABOUT LIFE!! I'M GONNA KILL HIM!!
PHILOSOPHERS OF THE NORTH!!

Just a daydream that began with that metaphor and the problem some tourists have with super energetic guides. I remember one big game guide, working out of Atlin, who prided himself on exhausting his clients. By the same token, northerners get frustrated with tourists who are always in a rush. I tried to combine all these themes in this strip plus a little dig at "biological nomenclature" (using two Latin names for every species).

DON'T BOTHER WITH ALL THAT STOVE PIPE CLEANING GEAR!
©D. URQUHART

OLD TIMERS JUST BUILT A ROARING FIRE TO BURN OUT THE CREOSOTE!
HARDWARE

SO! HAL! THAT OLD TIMER'S TRICK FIX YOUR PIPES?
SURE DID!!

CLEAN AS A @*✲ WHISTLE!!
97-42

This is an old northern joke I heard in Ft. Smith years ago. There used to be a product called "Red Devil" that you threw in the firebox to cause a mini chimney fire in order to burn out the soot and creosote. Don't see it around anymore.

WOW! A BULL GOING OVER THE HILL! HURRY AND WE'LL CATCH UP TO HIM!!!
BUT WHAT IF THERE'S...
BLAM! BLAM! BLAM! PING! TUNK! TUNK! HISSSS!!
97-43
...HUNTERS ON THE OTHER SIDE?!!
© D.URQUHART

97-44
WELL, THE WILDLIFE APPEARS TO HAVE THIS NO HUNTING CORRIDOR ALL FIGURED OUT!!
©D.URQUHART

5 DAYS AND NO BULLS CALLING BACK!
UNK! UNK! UNK!
CRACK
CRACK
WHAT'S A GUY HAFTA DO TO GET A MOOSE IN THIS
COUNTRY?!!!
© D.URQUHART
THIS BETTER WORK!!
97-45
WILD
WILDLIF HERITA
SAVE OUR WILDLIFE HABITATS
WILD SPACES
WILDLIFE IS FOR EVERYONE

Road hunting is the subject of endless debate in the north. People like the opportunity to jump in the truck after work or on the weekend and go hunting. But there are also negative impacts on wildlife and humans! Not long ago, a fellow in Dawson told me how he had changed his mind against no-hunting corridors because it created so much more snowmachine disturbance beyond the corridor. And so it goes.

The Dempster Highway cuts through the winter range of the Porcupine Caribou Herd. Over the past 20 years a variety of no-hunting corridors have been experimented with and recently a total no-hunting ban was imposed for one week based on traditional knowledge that the leaders of the herd should not be disturbed. Suddenly, caribou were seen all over the place and even became a local tourist attraction.

In the first panel, Marten is using three hunting methods simultaneously: calling, thrashing willows with a shoulder blade to simulate moose antlers, and pouring water into the lake to sound like peeing. I juxtaposed this image with the ardent conservationists with whom many northerners are uncomfortable, yet have to admit their effectiveness.

UH-OH! BEARS!!
ROGER! GRACE! YOU GUYS LOOK UM... SO SLEEK!!
ULP! YES! AND UM... ROTUND!!
97-46
©D.URQUHART

THANKS! I PUT ON 53 INCHES AND GRACE 49!!
BUT WE'RE GETTING SO SLEEPY!!
GOOD BERRY YEAR!

Every fall there are many discussions about what kind of berry year it has been and how it will affect the bears. In poor berry years, bears can become problems in communities.

AH! THE PRISTINE WILDERNESS! A LAND WITHOUT HUMANS!
WHAT DO YOU MEAN?

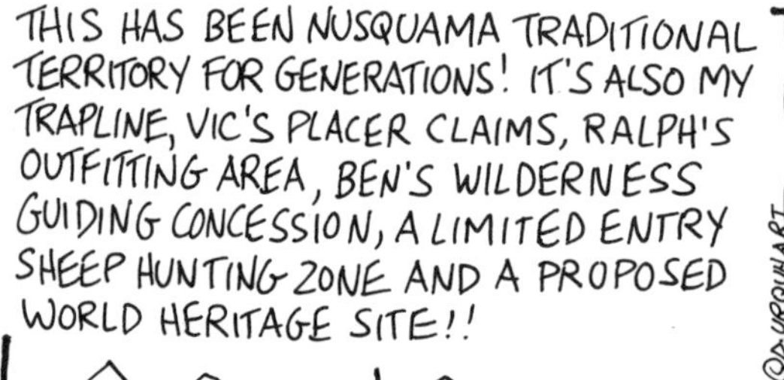
THIS HAS BEEN NUSQUAMA TRADITIONAL TERRITORY FOR GENERATIONS! IT'S ALSO MY TRAPLINE, VIC'S PLACER CLAIMS, RALPH'S OUTFITTING AREA, BEN'S WILDERNESS GUIDING CONCESSION, A LIMITED ENTRY SHEEP HUNTING ZONE AND A PROPOSED WORLD HERITAGE SITE!!
©D.URQUHART

YOU MEAN THERE'S NO SUCH THING AS WILDERNESS?!!
NEVER WAS!!
97-47

The concept of wilderness is a southern one. People who live in the bush don't see it as an empty land. The other day I heard that a B.C. First Nation petitioned the provincial government for the removal of a promotional quote by Captain Cook about the land only lacking people to inhabit it. Nusquama means "Nowhere" in Latin and was the original title for Thomas More's Utopia. The printer changed it to the Greek for "Nowhere" without telling him.

SO? WHAT PART OF THE SOUTH ARE YOU FROM?
ME?

I DON'T GET IT! I DRESS LIKE YOU DO! CUSS LIKE YOU DO! DRIVE A 4x4, CHEW SNOOSE AND DRINK BEER! BUT YOU STILL KNOW I'M A SOUTHERNER!
©D.URQUHART

WHAT GIVES ME AWAY?!!
YER WINDSHIELD!
97-48

This is based on a comment made by a Mayo trapper, Pete Beattie, at his 50th birthday party. He is caricatured in the strip on the far left. I've set out the original to give to him but he and his wife are always away in the bush!

WELL! STELLA'S HOUSE IS FINALLY DONE!
SHE BEGAN IT WITH LEN THE LOGGER! REMEMBER?
©D.URQUHART

THEN SHE LEFT HIM FOR CHUCK THE CARPENTER AND AFTER HIM WAS PETE THE PLUMBER, THEN DAN THE DRYWALLER AND NOW SHE'S WITH PAT THE PAINTER!

97-49
YESSIR! TOOK A LOT OF

SHACKING UP TO GET THAT BUILT!!

This is pretty much a true story from a northern community I know well. I doubt that it was this intentional but it fit the cliché of "shacking up" perfectly. Using such terms and presenting such material is a departure from southern strips that stick to more socially correct standards.

YOU ARE A GOD! G-O-D! AND I MUST OBEY!!
©D.URQUHART
SKOOKUM! SNAP OUT OF IT!!
I SAID YOU ARE A DOG D-O-G! AND YOU MUST OBEY!!

97-50
WATCH OUT FOR HORSE POOP WITH LITTLE RED MUSHROOMS IN THEM!!

I tinkered with this idea for years. Other versions I tried would surely have offended religious readers. In the 1970s, farmers on the west coast of B.C. and the islands were seriously bothered by hippies in their fields looking for little red mushrooms that grow on cow patties.

HEY GUYS! LET'S PLAYFIGHT!!!
NOT NOW SKOOK WE'RE BUSY...
©D.URQUHART 97-51

C'MON! PETER AND THE WOLF! I'M THE WOLF AND YOU'RE THE HUNTSMEN!
OKAY!

DA-DUH-DA DUH-DA-DA A RARRR!! DA-DUH-DA DUH! RARR RARRR!!!
BOOM! DEE DEE DEE DUM BOOM! BOOM!!

DUM-DUM-DEE-DUM DEE-DUM! DEE DUM DUM DUM!!!
ULP! I FORGOT HOW THIS ENDED!!

Many times I've noticed how bored sled dogs get when waiting for humans to finish their work and do something interesting. Often we'd stop and amuse them for a while. When living in the bush, I tried to think of ways to make our dogs help more with our workload. One year I built a huge treadmill and made our leader run inside it to power a rotary washing machine.

NO GAS FOR 200 MILES!? WHAT A SLEAZY NORTHERN LIE!!
NO GAS FOR 200 MILES
©D. URQUHART
HELP!
POPULATION 3.5 MILLION?! TYPICAL SOUTHERN BOAST!!
POPULATION 3,500,000
97-52
HELP

There's a story about a young man from Atlin who drove all the way to Vancouver for a look see but as the traffic became thicker and faster near the city he just turned around and drove home again. In panels 2 and 4, I tried to parallel the feelings of "hostile wilderness" and "concrete jungle" by making the mountain ranges and city buildings look the same.

SKOOKUM'S NORTHERN EVOLUTION
©D. URQUHART
97-53

SURVIVAL OF THE UNFITTEST

Growing on permafrost in an arctic desert, many of our trees are stunted and misshapen. You are never so much aware of this as at Christmas time. I applied Darwin's theory of natural selection in a Taoist paradox here (being useless is most useful) employing Herbert Spencer's term "Survival of the Fittest"

97-54
Heh! Heh! I GAVE THOSE NORTHERNERS A WORD THEY'VE NEVER HEARD OF!!

GRAY JAY? SECOND WORD!! JAY?
©D.R. URQUHART

WALKING? WALKING JAY? JAY WALKING? JAY WALKING!!

WHAT'S IT MEAN?
BEATS ME!!

An elder told me about the time in the 1970s he drove from Ft. McPherson to Inuvik and near the centre of town he found all the vehicles were stopped in his lane. So he pulled out and drove past them in the left lane. As he was crossing through the main intersection he noticed a red light hanging from a pole. He had no idea what it was for.

1997

"...As the limo moved onto the Interstate, he opened the liquor cabinet and said to her..."

CARE FOR SOME MOSSBERRY WINE AND THEN WE COULD GO UP TO THE LOFT...
© D. URQUHART

"It had been her toughest murder case and right now the male species filled her with mistrust, even the handsome D.A., so she replied ..."
97-55

(sigh)...THANKS, BUT NOT TONIGHT, I'VE... JUST GOT TOO MUCH ON MY MIND...
WHEN BUSH NOVELS COLLIDE!

After this strip came out, one person asked me if my wife minded me depicting our personal bush lives. In the social deprivation of isolated bush life you are influenced much more by any "external" stimulus. All day long as you are hunting, checking fish nets or getting firewood, you are thinking about the novel you're reading or what you heard on the radio.

GREAT CONFERENCE! BEAUTIFUL HOTEL!!
THANKS! I OWN IT

WELL YOU SURE THOUGHT OF EVERTHING!!
YOU AIN'T SUPRISED A GUY WHO LOOKS LIKE ME IS A MILLIONAIRE?

HELL! I'M FROM THE NORTH!!
EVERYONE LOOKS LIKE YOU!
© D. URQUHART
97-56

Northerners have a pretension about being unpretentious. Our uniform is the ball cap, mackinaw shirt, insulated vest, jeans and work boots. Big orange Husqvarna suspenders are a good touch. I've noticed that some modifications are creeping in. Particularly, faded cotton shirts, hiking boots and fleeces. But the studied casualness is still there and has been adopted even by our bureaucrats.

Outside

1998

OH! MY GOD!!

"Going outside" is a term from another era but the feelings of fear and loathing still apply.

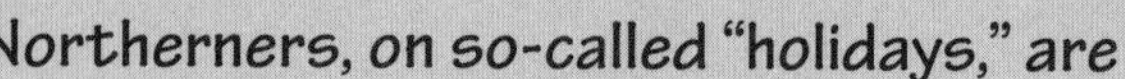

97-52
HELP

Northerners, on so-called "holidays," are

often stunned by face-to-face encounters with southern congestion, pollution and frenzy. If anything, it confirms their worst fears about the "crazy world out there" and renews their devotion to the north as the haven it truly is.

AND WE'RE JUST
COMING HOME!!

INNIE!
OUTIE!
98-1

A BUCK?
YOU'RE ON!

YOU WIN! AGAIN!!
AND YOU NEVER LEARN IF IT'S A BRIEFCASE IT'S USUALLY AN OUTIE!
AND I HAVE NO IDEA WHAT THEY ARE TALKING ABOUT!!

I was only accustomed to the terms "innie" and "outie" for belly buttons until a woman in Atlin referred to parka hoods this way. I then realized that an important component in my assessment of any stranger is whether they have an "innie" or an "outie." My feeling is that bush types usually have "innies" because they use their hoods more and do not want them to be covered with snow or needles and little branches.

SKRIK! CRACKLE! CRICKLE! CRACKLE

CAN'T YOU WALK QUIETER? YOU SOUND LIKE YOU'RE MADE OF CELLOPHANE!!
IT'S THIS NEW ULTRA LIGHTWEIGHT MATERIAL! IT GETS BRITTLE AT 30 BELOW!!
CRICKLE, CRICK! CRICK!
98-2

SO? EVER WONDER WHY YOUR WINTER SURVEYS ALWAYS SHOW A DECLINE IN WILDLIFE POPULATIONS??
CRICK! CRACKLE! CRACK! CRICKLE!

Modern bush gear always looks so great in the civilized recreational stores but it may function differently in the bush. Hunters often complain about the crackle of their new gear once the temperature drops.

LAST TIME IT CAME DOWN LIKE THIS MY DAD'S HUSKIES...

KEPT MOVING UP AS THE SNOW ROSE UNTIL THEIR CHAINS WERE TAUT AND...

BY MORNING ALL HE COULD FIND WAS THEIR NOSES POKING OUT!!!
©D. URQUHART 98-3

WELL! HAVE A GOOD SLEEP!

This is an old story I picked up in the Mackenzie Delta 30 years ago. I recently shipped a "wall tent" like this one to the Canadian Embassy in Washington. It got stopped at customs because nobody knew what a "wall tent" was.

I MUST LEAVE YOU NOW AND GO TO THE PLACE OF SMOKING HOODS!
I THINK OLD RALPH HAS BEEN SPENDING TOO MUCH TIME WITH YOU IN THE COMMUNITIES!!
DON'T WORRY! IT'S JUST SOME BUSH CODE HE PICKED UP FOR...
A CIGARETTE BREAK AT A GOVERNMENT OFFICE WHEN IT'S 35 BELOW!
© D. URQUHART
98-4

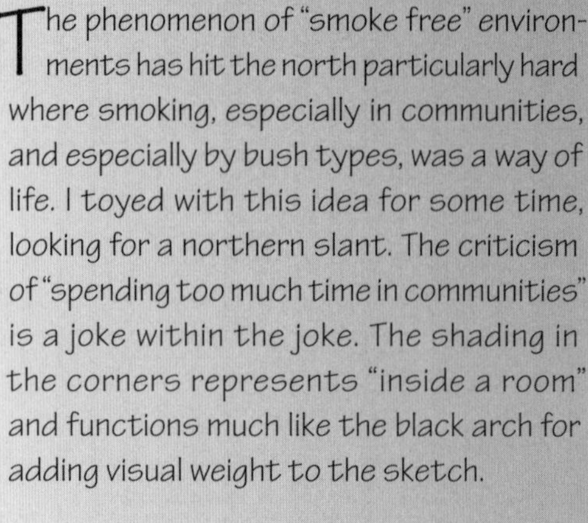

The phenomenon of "smoke free" environments has hit the north particularly hard where smoking, especially in communities, and especially by bush types, was a way of life. I toyed with this idea for some time, looking for a northern slant. The criticism of "spending too much time in communities" is a joke within the joke. The shading in the corners represents "inside a room" and functions much like the black arch for adding visual weight to the sketch.

MY GOD! MARTEN'S BOUGHT A SKIDOO!!!
SKIDOO
98-5
AND HE'S GOT A KNIFE! HE'S GOING TO KILL US!!!
SLASH!!
STAB!!!
SLICE!!
©D. URQUHART
HEY! HEY! WHAT'S THE MATTER WITH YOU DOGS??!!

Back when I lived in Sachs Harbour there was an annual sea lift at which time you got your yearly food and other supplies all at once. Fox trappers were quite wealthy back then and one guy had ordered a special "Peterborough" boat built to his own design. A few hours after it was unpacked, kids, playing in the carton, set fire to the box and burned up the boat as well.

ELDERS SAY IT HASN'T BEEN THIS WARM SINCE THEY WERE KIDS!!
POLLUTION!! GLOBAL WARMING!! THE CURSE OF OUR MODERN WORLD!!!
OH YEAH? SO WHY WAS IT THIS WARM 80 YEARS AGO?
WELL ... IT'S ... BECAUSE ... THAT IS ... YOU ... YOU NORTHERNERS DON'T UNDERSTAND SCIENCE!!!
98-6
AND WE GET CONFUSED BY MORE THAN A GENERATION'S WORTH OF DATA!!
©D. URQUHART

It's only through our modern technology which measures everything that we have to fear global warming. But from analysing glaciers and bog cores, science also provides a long view showing the earth is always cycling through climatic changes. This is also what traditional knowledge shows. So what's the big deal? "Oh! But it's happening a lot faster!" they say. Always something to worry about.

AND OUR PROJECT WILL INCORPORATE TRADITIONAL KNOWLEDGE!
GREAT!
YEAH! GREAT!
REALLY GREAT!

BUT WHAT EXACTLY IS TRADITIONAL KNOWLEDGE?

©D. URQUHART

98-7
IT'S GREAT!
YEAH! GREAT!
REALLY GREAT!

This has been one of my most popular strips in recent years. Recognition of aboriginal rights has introduced an array of "new" principles to our society that civil servants must now pay lip service to. I always draw them connected in a black mass with arms poking out as if they were all part of one creature.

IN RUSSIA THEY SLIDE DOWN ONION DOMES AND WEAR THE GOLD OFF...

IN MICHIGAN THEY PULL UP FISHING LINES AND EAT THE BAIT...

IN INUVIK THEY SHIELD THE PHOTOCELL TO TURN ON STREET LIGHTS AND WARM THEIR TOES...
©D. URQUHART

98-8
WHAT DO YOUR RAVENS DO??

The first two panels come from an article in *Sports Illustrated* that I read years ago. The Inuvik observation I often made while passing through that town to my home in Sachs Harbour.

98-9
ANOTHER THAW AND MY TIPS WILL BE TOAST!!!
TOO LITTLE SNOW! DRY SPRING!! BIG FOREST FIRES ARE COMING!!!
CLEAR CUTS ON THAT MOUNTAIN SOUTH OF US!!
TOO MUCH WIND!
I SAW A SPRUCE BEETLE ON YOU LAST FALL!!
THE BEAVERS ARE BACK!!
I GOT BLAZED FOR A MINING CLAIM THIS WINTER!!
ANTS IN MY HEARTWOOD! I'M LEAKING SAWDUST!!

AH! THE PEACEFUL UNTROUBLED SERENITY OF THE NORTHERN FOREST!!
©D. URQUHART

People who spend brief times in the bush see it as a beautiful backdrop to a day in the great outdoors. When you live in the bush and gradually merge into other frames of reference, "tree time" for instance, your surroundings come alive in a new and dynamic way. Bush life is still very tranquil in some respects but in others, even a quiet forest can appear like a swirl of activity.

OKAY NOW! PUSH 2!
98-10

GOTTA HAND IT TO YOU J.B.!!

PUTTING AN ELEVATOR IN THIS TWO STOREY NORTHERN CENTRE SEEMED STUPID TO ME...

1 2

BUT EVERY FAMILY FROM THE BUSH COMMUNITIES BRINGS THEIR KIDS TO RIDE IT!!
©D. URQUHART

When we lived in Atlin — a community of 300 people, no traffic lights and a few two-storey buildings — a trip to Whitehorse was full of strange sites and experiences for our young children. Riding the elevator was one of them and could not to missed.

Blah... Blah... Blah... ...Blah... Blah...
ANOTHER HOUR OF THIS WORKSHOP THEN A BIG DINNER, HOT-TUB, MINIBAR, X-MOVIE...

...AND TONIGHT YOU'LL BREAK INTO COMMITTEES TO RESOLVE THE PROBLEMS WE HAVE IDENTIFIED
98-11

THIS MAY COME AS A SUPRISE TO THOSE WHO NEVER READ THE AGENDA WHICH SHOWS THIS IS A...

HOMEWORK SHOP!!

As a workshop facilitator over the past 10 years, I've learned to spot these guys. And sometimes I do assign homework!

WELL, WITH YOUR PROMOTION, THE NEW BEAMER AND OUR PACIFIC CRUISE...
98-12
WE SHOULD BE THE CONVERSATION CENTRE PIECE ALL EVENING!!
THEN ROSIE THREW A POT AT THE GRIZZLY! I FELL OFF THE ROOF AND THE HUSKIES...

Every northern couple who visits relatives down south will recognize this situation. Even explaining the most regular activities can hold a southern audience spellbound. As for the common question, "But why do you live there?" a number of people told me they just give people my other book, *Skookum's North*, and say, "That's why!"

OKAY! IF THE HEAD'S STUCK, YOU FLIP THE WHOLE THING UP AND OVER AND BRING IT...
DOWN! **LIKE THIS!!** NOW YOU TRY!!
AH! -AH! -AH! -AHH!
CRICK!
CRACK!!!
SNAP!
POP!
DID I MENTION MY AUNT'S A CHIROPRACTOR?
98-13
©D. URQUHART

I was looking at a spinal chart in a chiropractor's office after splitting some firewood this way. Surprisingly, many people do not know this technique. But I was in the office for other reasons. So there!

WE'VE NEVER HAD A NORTHERNER ON THE BARCELONA BIODIVERSITY PANEL BEFORE! TELL ME WHAT IS YOUR PERSONAL EXPERTISE WITH BIG GAME SPECIES OR CHARISMATIC MEGAFAUNA AS WE LIKE TO CALL THEM?
98-14

I STALK THEM! I SHOOT THEM! I EAT THEM!
AHEM!...SO! I HEAR YOU'RE AN EXPERT ON MICE, VOLES AND SHREWS OR ENIGMATIC MICROFAUNA AS WE ON THE BIODIVERSITY PANEL LIKE TO CALL THEM!!

A friend of mine came back outraged from one of these pompous international conferences in Barcelona. He was disgusted by the smug academic detachment and superficial understanding of the participants, plus the lack of concern about nothing getting accomplished. The terms "mega" and "micro" fauna were coined by researchers annoyed with society's preoccupation with large attractive wildlife species.

COW MOOSE LIKE THIS PLACE!
AH-HA! **LOCAL DATA!!**
CHIEF TOLD ME!!
BINGO!! TRADITIONAL KNOWLEDGE!!
NO! NO! INDIGENOUS KNOWLEDGE!
HE'S A PROSPECTOR!
98-15
UH-OH! COULD BE **BUSH LORE?!**
WHAT WAS IT HE JUST TOLD US?
BEATS ME!!
I...I! FORGOT!!
©D. URQUHART

As chair of the Yukon Fish and Wildlife Management Board's Traditional Knowledge Working Group, I receive many academic papers on the subject which dissect this branch of learning to death and pontificate about it, without any real appreciation of its value or intent for its use.

MAN AM I HUNGRY!! THINK I'LL GRAB ME A TRAPPER!!
OH NO YOU DON'T!
98-16

WH...WH WHY?!!
BECAUSE I'VE WATCHED OVER 4 GENERATIONS ON THIS TRAPLINE!!
©D.URQUHART

AND THAT'S MY HUMAN!! I OWN HIM!!!

BIG BEAR COUNTRY HERE SKOOK!! BUT FUNNY THING IS I NEVER HAD A PROBLEM WITH ONE!!
THE TREES KNOW YOU!!

This is a Teslin Tlingit elders' saying. There are many trees around the cabin my wife and I built 26 years ago that I know personally and I feel they must know me.

BOY AM I BEAT!!
JUST ONE BAG TO GO!!

OKAY! 30% RECYCLABLES NOT RECYCLED! 42% COMPOSTIBLES NOT COMPOSTED, 10% TOXICS NOT SENT TO PROPER DISPOSAL!
©D.URQUHART

THIS RESEARCH IS REALLY TOUGH!!
YEAH! BUT SOMEBODY'S GOT TO DO IT!!!
98-17

AND I BET THEY THINK WE EAT THIS CRUD!!!

Our local recycling centre in Whitehorse is called "Raven Recycling." At the dump in Atlin there is a drawing of a raven on a sign that says, "Randy Raven says please push your garbage over the edge!"

SPRING TIME!! I HUNT DUCKS NOW!
YEP! I KNOW!

YOU DON'T ARREST ME!!
NOPE!
©D.URQUHART

YOU MADE A BIG MISTAKE! YOU FIXED IT!
YEP!

COME FOR DUCK SOUP!
HE JUST THANKED YOU!
YEP! I KNOW!
98-18

The original 1916 Migratory Bird Treaty between Canada and the United States prohibited spring waterfowl hunting and started the fall season so late that the birds were mostly gone from the arctic before the season began. This was a constant hardship for Inuit and First Nations but only after land claims were settled in the Western Arctic did they have the resources to fight the process. Recently, the treaty has been amended to permit more realistic hunting activities in the north.

98-19
I'M WORRIED ABOUT THIS OPEN HOUSE!! NOBODY RETURNS MY CALLS! NOBODY IS MAKING PREPARATIONS!
RELAX! WE TALKED TO SOME PEOPLE! THEY KNOW WHAT TO DO!!
©D.URQUHART
OH! I SEE! SO I JUST SIT BACK AND SOMEHOW THROUGH THE MYSTERIOUS CHANNELS OF YOUR TIGHT LITTLE BUSH COMMUNITY MAGIC WILL HAPPEN!!
YEP IT WILL!
OR... THEN AGAIN MAYBE IT WON'T
STAY CALM! KEEP STRONG AND WAIT FOR THE SIGNS!!

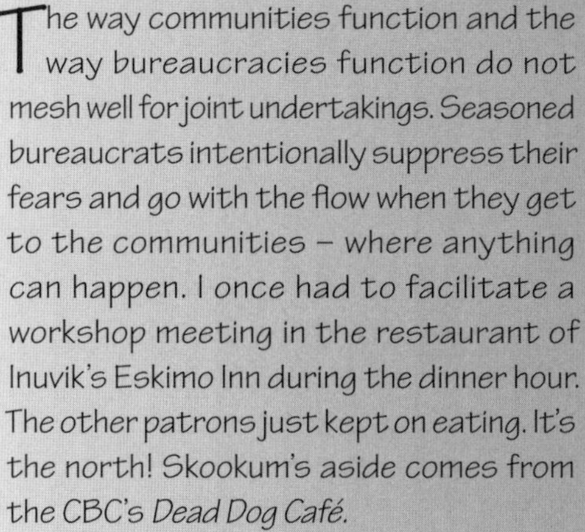

The way communities function and the way bureaucracies function do not mesh well for joint undertakings. Seasoned bureaucrats intentionally suppress their fears and go with the flow when they get to the communities – where anything can happen. I once had to facilitate a workshop meeting in the restaurant of Inuvik's Eskimo Inn during the dinner hour. The other patrons just kept on eating. It's the north! Skookum's aside comes from the CBC's *Dead Dog Café.*

98-20
SO? DO WE HAVE ENOUGH STYROFOAM CUPS AND PLASTIC CUTLERY FOR THE ENVIRONMENTAL OPEN HOUSE?
ISN'T PLASTIC A BAD CHOICE FOR AN ENVIRONMENTAL GATHERING?!!
WE COULD BRING STUFF FROM HOME AND HAVE A BIG CLEAN-UP AFTER!!
©D.URQUHART
WELL, MARTEN! I THINK WE'VE GOT ENOUGH CUPS LEFT OVER FROM THE POTLUCK!!
AND I'LL BRING PLASTIC CUTLERY FROM THE MINER'S PICNIC!!

This comes directly from comments made during a workshop planning session in Mayo, Yukon.

98-21
THIS IS GONNA BE ONE HECKUVA PUBLIC MEETING!!
©D.URQUHART

The north is a society of passionate individualists. Public meetings are often very emotional and, since they can easily be dominated by an aggressive and vocal minority, are not a great means for achieving consensus or getting an in-depth understanding of opinions.

THANKYOU SO MUCH FOR YOUR IMPASSIONED SPEECH ABOUT THE WILDERNESS!! YOU SAVED THIS UNIQUE AND PRECIOUS AREA!!
98-22

YES! YOU ARE THE HERO OF THE DAY!!

YOU CRAZY FOOL!! YOU JUST LOCKED UP A TREASURE OF RESOURCES AND THE CHANCE FOR JOBS AND PROSPERITY FOR THE NORTH!!

ONE CANNOT WALK ON WATER ON ALL LAKES!!
© D. URQUHART

This comment was made to me by Christine Lee, the Executive Director of a southern charitable foundation. It typifies the difficulty of making any development decisions that are highly charged, both economically and environmentally. I recently saw an enlargement of this in the coffee room of the Yukon's Renewable Resources department.

THESE DRUMS HAVE BEEN LEAKING HERE FOR 10 ✯@ YEARS!
HOW MANY LETTERS HAVE WE WRITTEN ABOUT THEM?!!

AND WE PUT THEM ON EVERY CLEAN-UP PROPOSAL!!
THAT NEVER GOT FUNDING!!

WELL.. UM, WE COULD LOAD THEM INTO YOUR TRUCK AND TAKE THEM TO THE DUMP?
98-23
© D. URQUHART

TELL YOU WHAT!! I'LL FAX THE @✯!! GOVERNMENT AND WE'LL PICKET THEIR OFFICES AND CALL THE MEDIA!! THAT'LL GET ACTION!!

In the good old days, the north was a playground for the military and industry. In the 1970s, the north came out of its slumber and people began to agitate for respect and change. During the '80s and '90s, much of this effort was directed at blaming big government and industry, to the point where individual initiative almost disappeared. Nowadays, there are more local clean-up campaigns and some kind of balance is being restored.

WHY THANK... OH! YOUR POOR HANDS!! WHAT HAPPENED TO THEM?!!
CRACKS FROM COLD... GREASE FROM ENGINES... CUTS FROM SKINNING... I WORK WITH MY HANDS!
98-24
© D. URQUHART

REAL WORKING HANDS!!
SO RUGGED! SO STRONG!
SO COARSE! SO ROUGH!!
SHOULD I SHOW THEM WHERE THE BEAR BIT ME?

In 1970, I lived at a seismic camp on Banks Island. The camp mechanic's hands looked like gloves, they were so cracked with cold and embedded with grease from working under equipment at down to -50°C. He claimed gloves were too clumsy for the precise work he had to do. It's always comforting when, at community planning sessions, I look around the table and see several cracked and greasy hands sifting through the stacks of papers.

RENTAL CAR QUIT! WE'LL MISS OUR PLANE!!
WE'LL HITCH!

BUT SIR! THIS IS THE CITY!! NO ONE WILL PICK US UP!!
©D. URQUHART
98-25

NOT EVERYONE IN THE CITY IS FROM THE CITY!!
I TRAP NORTH OF MOOSEBERRY MYSELF!!

Several years ago in mid-winter, I had to get the 110 miles from Whitehorse back to my home in Atlin. A friend offered to drive me but I just made a cardboard sign and was home in 4 hours. In Alaska, when it is below -40°F, it is against the law to not pick up hitchhikers.

TOO SHORT FOR BASKETBALL...

TOO LIGHT FOR HOCKEY AND FOOTBALL...

TOO WIREY FOR WEIGHTS! TOO IMPATIENT FOR CURLING...

98-26
BUT JUST RIGHT FOR THE BUSH!!
© D. URQUHART
©D. URQUHART

I've always been actively involved in a variety of sports but am often disadvantaged by my physique. In the bush I feel right at home. I'm just the right size. I imagine many others feel the same way.

WOOD FLOATS! THAT'S WHY WOOD BOATS FLOAT!!
METAL DON'T FLOAT! BUT STEEL SHIPS DO?!!
98-27

FEATHERS ARE LIGHT! THAT'S WHY BIRDS CAN FLY!!
BUT WHAT ABOUT PLANES MADE OF ALUMINUM?
©D. URQUHART

WE HAVE NO @☆* IDEA WHAT WE'RE TALKING ABOUT!!!
STAY IN SCHOOL!!

In 1972, I was living in Ft. Smith, NWT and a friend, who was feeding his sled dogs on an island in the Slave River, overheard two oldtimers by the shore marvelling at the miracle of jet flight. I just expanded on his story.

FRITZ! I SEE A BEAR!!! ... READY?!!
YA!!!
PSSST!! PSSST!!
©D.URQUHART 98-28
AHHH!!
AHHH!!
WHAT THE HECK?!! I CAN'T EAT BOTH OF THEM!!!

I have heard this story several times. It could be a "northern myth" like the "urban myths" about alligators in sewer systems. One day they evacuated the entire Department of Renewable Resources due to an unidentified toxic leak. Turned out to be a can of bear spray in one of the biologists' offices.

OIL PRICES HAVE REALLY DROPPED LATELY!!
RIGHT!
©D.URQUHART
98-29

SO HOW COME WE DON'T SEE LOWER PRICES AT THE PUMP?
WELL, THOSE RATES ARE GENERATED DOWN SOUTH AND IT TAKES AWHILE FOR FLUCTUATIONS TO WORK THEIR WAY NORTH

IT'S REALLY TOO COMPLICATED FOR NORTHERNERS TO UNDERSTAND!
YOU MEAN LIKE HOW THE CEO OF EXXON GOT A SIX MILLION DOLLAR BONUS THIS YEAR?
Gouge: A word of Celtic origin meaning to swindle or extort money from

Just as this book is going to press, oil prices have surged again. This cyclical debate has been going on since the early '70s but finding the true cause and culprits is like nailing jello to a wall.

Dear Mr. Marten:
I am hitchinghiker from last summer! You are pleased to be finding me log cabin on trapline for living free bush life cheap off the land!
Truly Sincere,
Herman
P.S. I have $600
©D.URQUHART 98-30

DEAR HERMAN:
COST OF TRAPLINE 42,000
COST OF CABIN 8,000
AIR CHARTER TO LAKE 2,500
1 YEAR GRUB 2,800
COST OF TRAPS 3,200
COST OF SLED & DOGS 6,000
COST OF CANOE/MOTOR 7,200
COST OF GUN & AMMO 850
COST OF CAMP GEAR 2,300
MINUS (600)
YOU ONLY NEED $74,250
Marten

A nice young European came to Atlin for a winter. Naturally we called him "Herman the German." Several years after returning to his country he wrote to me asking that I find him a cheap cabin as he was coming back to live here. I never did anything about it and he returned only for a brief visit anyway.

OUCH! OUCH! OUCH!!
98-31

OUCH! THE CANOE KEEPS BANGING THE BUTTON ON MY BALLCAP!
GOOD GRIEF! ARE YOU NORTHERNERS SO VAIN YOU CAN **NEVER** REMOVE YOUR HATS?!!
©D.URQUHART

OUCH! OUCH! OUCH! OUCH! OUCH!
LUCKY THE VOYAGEURS ONLY HAD TOQUES!!

This is me under the canoe. There is really no place to put your ball cap for a quick portage. No, really, there isn't. Being bald has nothing to do with it!

WHERE'S OUR GUIDE NOW?!!
DUNNO! MAYBE AHEAD ON THE TRAIL!!

THE BUSH REALLY SCARES ME! I'LL BE SO RELIEVED WHEN WE SEE HIM AGAIN!

WELL DON'T LET ON! THAT'S JUST WHAT THESE SILLY CHILDISH NORTHERNERS LOVE!

I FEEL SO CHILDISH!!
AND SO SILLY!!
98-32
©D.URQUHART

This strip covers several themes. One: northerners are at home in the bush and southerners stick to trails. Two: the bush brings out the kid in you. Three: there is something about tourists' naïve vulnerability that prompts this kind of prank.

I CAN'T FIGURE IF RAVENS HAVE NO SENSE OF SMELL OR ARE JUST INCREDIBLY STUPID!!
WHY?
98-33

WELL, YOU'RE STANDING BESIDE A ROTTEN, MAGGOT INFESTED JACKFISH AND EITHER YOU CAN'T SMELL IT OR....
©D.URQUHART

YOU HAVEN'T GOT BRAINS ENOUGH TO **ROLL IN IT!!**

Everyday we walk our dog in the bush. Even at a great distance I can tell from his posture what he is contemplating and I shout at the top of my voice, "DON'T EVEN THINK ABOUT IT!"

BOY! YOU'VE TRAVELLED ALL OVER THE NORTH! HOW DO YOU KEEP YOUR RV SO NEAT AND CLEAN?
WE DON'T HIKE!
HIKING'S MESSY!
WE DON'T BOAT!
BOATING'S MESSY!!
WE DON'T FISH!!
FISHING'S VERY MESSY!
WE DON'T COOK OUT!
CAMPFIRE'S ARE MESSY!
LOOKS TO ME LIKE THEY 'Messed' THE WHOLE POINT OF TRAVELLING!!
98-34

A good friend of mine from Ft. McPherson, Johnny Charlie Sr., who recently passed away, told me about some tourists he invited to his place for tea. To get such an invitation, especially from an ex-chief and famous personality was their good fortune but the couple said, "No thanks! We've got everything here in our RV!" Johnny wondered why they bothered to come north at all if they spent all their time in their own spaceship.

THESE ARE VERY SENSITIVE PEOPLE SO JUST TRY TO BLEND IN!!
25TH ANNUAL CONSERVATION CONFERENCE

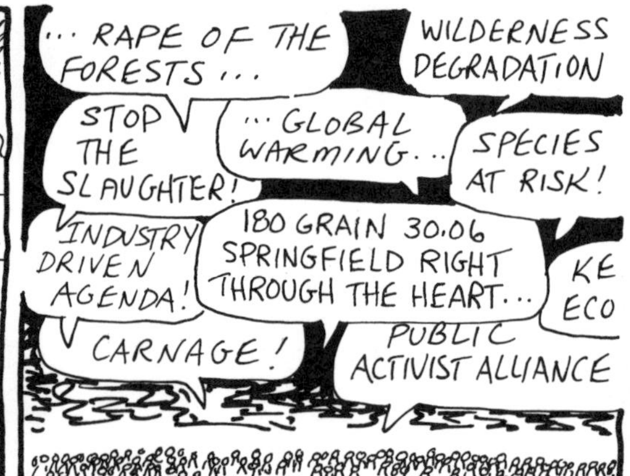
... RAPE OF THE FORESTS ...
WILDERNESS DEGRADATION
STOP THE SLAUGHTER!
... GLOBAL WARMING ...
SPECIES AT RISK!
INDUSTRY DRIVEN AGENDA!
180 GRAIN 30.06 SPRINGFIELD RIGHT THROUGH THE HEART...
KE ECO
CARNAGE!
PUBLIC ACTIVIST ALLIANCE

WHAT GAVE ME AWAY?
25TH ANNUAL Conservation Conference
98-35

I drew this to contrast the rhetoric of the international conservation lobby and the practical attitudes of northerners. Even when they are on the same side, each group treats the other with polite suspicion. It's hard to provide a number of separate speeches in a strip so one solution is to minimize or remove the speakers entirely.

EVER WONDER WHY THEY CALL THIS BARK FUNGUS??
98-36

WATCH!
WOOF! WOOF! WOOF! WOOF!

IT'S A LIVING!

As in strip 98-32, the gullibility of tourists is a constant temptation for northern guides to indulge in harmless mischief.

YOU ARE LIKINK ZEE BELGIAN VAFFLES?
UNT ZEE BAVARIAN CHOCOLATE COFFEE MIT SPRINKLES?

WELL, I ALWAYS WANTED TO GO TO EUROPE!
BUT INSTEAD...
ITALIA CANOE RENTA

EUROPE CAME TO US!!!
98-37
EUROPA HOTEL
SWISS CHOCOLATE SHOP
GERMAN BAKERY
WHITE WATE RAFTING TOUR
WIR SPRECHEN
©D.URQUHART

I drew this after dining at the "Raven," an internationally recognized gourmet restaurant in the small town of Haines Junction, Yukon. At the gas station down the road I was served by a very polite older Swiss gentleman. Parked nearby was a classic Mercedes tour bus (shown in panel 3).

ULP! THERE'S AXEL THE KILLER DOG! I HAVE TO RUSH HIM OR HE'LL KNOW I'M SCARED?!!
98-38

IF ONLY MARTEN WOULD CALL ME!! PLEASE GOD!! PLEASE GOD!! PLEASE GOD!!!
©D.URQUHART

SKOOKUM! GET THE @☆*!!! BACK HERE NOW!
NO PROBLEMO!
THANKS BUD!

I drew this after pondering why my gentle-natured husky, "Cisco," becomes so aggressive around bigger dogs but ignores smaller ones. I have actually bailed him out of similar situations.

THE CHIEF SAYS HIS YOUTHFUL LOOKS ARE NOTHING BUT BARE GRECIAN FORMULA!!
98-39

NOW WHAT KIND OF TRADITIONAL MEDICINE IS THAT?
©D.URQUHART

ACTUALLY I SAID "NOTHING

BUT BEAR GREASE IN FORMULA"!

This came from a joke made by Georgina Sydney, a Tlingit woman who is on our Traditional Knowledge Working Group of the Yukon Fish and Wildlife Management Board. It touches on the still prevalent skepticism about the value and authenticity of traditional knowledge.

SKOOKUM'S
DOG
DICTIONARY
VOL. 1

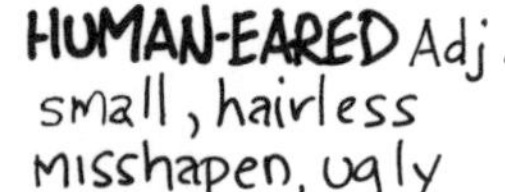
HUMAN-EARED Adj.
small, hairless
misshapen, ugly

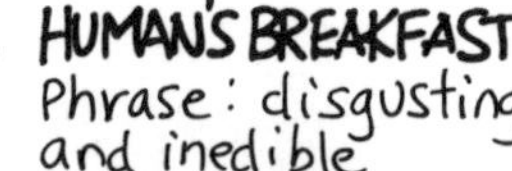
HUMAN'S BREAKFAST
Phrase: disgusting
and inedible

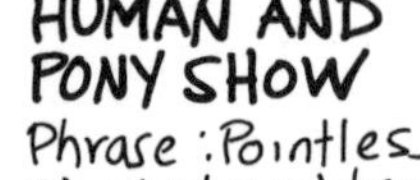
HUMAN AND
PONY SHOW
Phrase: Pointless
physical punishment
and animal torture

HUMAN
DAYS adj.

Time
wasted
in frantic
rushing
about

© D. URQUHART
98-40

Think of all our insulting dog sayings: Dog-eat-dog, Dog's life, Doggonit, Dirty Dog, Dog's body (British), Dog-in-the-manger…

AND IF YOU TAKE THIS JOB THE COMPANY WILL GIVE

YOU AND YOUR FAMILY A FREE TRIP DOWN SOUTH!!

© D. URQUHART 98-41

DO WE HAVE TO GO?!!

Years ago the "packages" to entice southerners to work up north were stunning. Subsidized housing and fuel, medical and dental plans, free holiday flights, northern allowance, isolation pay. Vestiges of it are still around, the message being, "You'll hate it here and it's just a temporary career move but we need you!" Naturally, locals, who are struggling to get by because they love the north and want to stay here, feel a certain resentment towards this double standard.

98-42

© D. URQUHART
YES!
YES!!
YES!!
CLUNK!

RADIO MARS IMMEDIATELY! WE'VE DISCOVERED ROCKS ON EARTH!!

I drew this after another gushing in the media about extraterrestrial life. In January, 2000, I saw a huge meteor streak across the sky right over Whitehorse. NASA came up and there was a frenzy to find a fragment that might shed light on our origins. Eventually a local found a piece and I just heard that it is rich in amino acids. Oh joy! Again we prostrate ourselves in the likeness of our own image. Oh, well, science is our religion and the universe is all about us, isn't it?

WE GOT TWO HOURS! LET'S GO! GO! GO!!
98-43
OKAY! TIME'S UP!!!
WELL, THAT WAS SUMMER!
WELCOME TO THE NORTH!
©D. URQUHART

A hot, calm, sunny summer day is the cause for much excitement in the north. It's almost so precious you don't know what to do with it so you try and do everything and feel frustrated all the time when you should just be enjoying it.

OH NO! IT'S THAT STUPID MOOSE CALLING CONTEST AGAIN!!
BUNCH OF CITY AMATEURS! NEVER SHOT A MOOSE IN THEIR LIFE!
AAAH-AAAHHH
UNK! UNK!

WHERE DO THEY GET THESE PEOPLE ANYWAYS? HAR! HAR! HAR!
THAT GUY SOUNDS LIKE..

98-44
A DYING PIG!! HAR! HAR! HAR!
UNK! UNK!
AAAH-AAAH AAA-HAAA
©D. URQUHART

Every fall there is a Canada-wide moose-calling contest on the radio. Northerners are understandably smug about their hunting prowess and apt to scoff at others.

WOW! TWO BIG BULLS!!
98-45
THAT'S A TON OF BUTCHERING!

FORTUNATELY YOU BROUGHT MY BOX OF TRUSTY... CARPENTRY TOOLS?!!
OOPS! WRONG BOX?
TAKES A LOT TO BREAK A NORTHERNER...

SO? GOOD HUNT BOYS?
NO! VIC! HE... WAAAAHH! WAAHH!!
NOT MY (SNIFF!) FAULT! I ONLY.. BAAA! HAA! HAA!!
BUT CUTTING UP TWO MOOSE WITH TIN SNIPS AND A CHISEL WILL DO IT!!

Plenty of these stories. A Tagish elder told me his excuse for butchering a whole moose with a small clasp knife. "I never expected to get one that day!" The tool box reference is to people who use river boats or freighter canoes for work and have various plywood boxes for grub, tools, camp gear, etc.

1998

WOW! THREE GAME TRAILS MERGED IN TO ONE HUMUNGOUS GAME TRAIL!
THIS MUST LEAD TO SOMETHING...
YIYYY!!
A GAME TRAIL THAT LEADS OVER A CLIFF? I DON'T GET IT?
A GUY WOULD DROP RIGHT OFF IF HE WASN'T CAREFUL!!
THAT'S THE "GAME" STUPID!!
98-46
© D. URQUHART

Some people don't get this one. It's a play on words "game trail." In this case the "game" made a "game." Not funny?

OH! MARTEN! THAT WHITE SHIRT SURE SETS OFF YOUR GORGEOUS TAN!!!
YEP! HE LOOKS JUST LIKE A BRAND NEW WALL TENT...

98-47
WITH A RUSTY OLD STOVE PIPE COMING OUT THE TOP!
© D. URQUHART
AND THUS THE ALPHA FEMALE ASSERTS HER DOMINANCE OVER HER MATE!!

This is a joke a Vuntut Gwich'in elder made about himself when I complimented him on his new shirt. But I felt the strip needed more of an ending. Skookum's remark refers to a recent study undertaken by a female researcher that shows wolf packs are actually lead by an "alpha" female.

JORDAN WILL COME BACK! AND RODMAN! SCOTTIE'S INJURIES MAKE HIM A POOR FREE AGENT! AND PHIL'S GONNA GO TO L.A. OR HOUSTON!
WHAT ABOUT THE JAZZ?

STOCKTON AND MALONE STILL HAVE A YEAR ON THEIR CONTRACTS SO I'D LOOK FOR A RETURN MATCH WITH CHICAGO!
BOY! YOU SURE KNOW YOUR STUFF!!
YEAH! FOR A GUY WHO'S NEVER PLAYED BASKETBALL OR BEEN WITHIN 1000 MILES OF AN NBA GAME!!
NORTHERN REVENGE!

WELL HELL! I GOT 15 SPORT CHANNELS ON THE DISH!!
AN ARCTIC SPORTS BAR EXPERT ON THE SOUTH!!
98-48

I love hearing local experts expound on sports trades and strategies as if they had insider information, instead of living in a place so remote nobody's ever heard of it. It's just as silly as southerners, like Farley Mowat, writing about the north.

THIS TRAIL SUCKS!
TELL MARTEN!
98-49

I'M NOT CLEARING THAT TRAIL! I DON'T TRAP THERE ANYMORE! IT'S IN THE NEW PARK!!
©D. URQUHART

BUT YOU CREATED A HISTORIC TRAIL!
AND THE NEW PARK POLICY SAYS IDENTIFY, DESIGNATE AND MAINTAIN HISTORIC TRAILS!!

NEXT TIME WE'RE SCOUTING BOUNDARIES FOR THE NEW PARK, KEEP YOUR MOUTH SHUT OKAY?!!

AND RAVEN DROPPED BEAVER FROM WAY UP HIGH AND WHEN HE HIT THE GROUND IT MADE THIS LAKE!!
98-50

10,000 YEARS AGO AN ICE CUBE THE SIZE OF MANHATTAN SAT HERE AND MELTED FOR 2,000 MORE YEARS CREATING THIS LAKE AND ESKERS OF STRATIFIED BOULDERS!

SO? WHAT DO YOU THINK, VIC?
WELL THE ICE CUBE SOUNDS PRETTY FAR FETCHED TO ME!
ME TOO! I GO WITH CHARLIE FRED JOHN'S VERSION!
©D. URQUHART

WELL THE NORTH WILL BACK THE BOREALIS PARTY THIS TIME!
HOW CAN YOU BE SO SURE?
F P B
6 1 12
8 3 27
5 1 2
3 4 2
©D. URQUHART

WE HAVE A POLLSTER IN FT. DOGGEREL NAMED FISHER WHO'S NEVER WRONG!
BUT WE DON'T KNOW HOW HE DOES IT!!

OKAY! AT THE JUNCTION ITS 45 BULLET HOLES FOR PROGRESS, 26 FOR FUTURE AND 12 FOR BOREALIS!
PROGRESS IS MONEY
YOUR VOTE IS YOUR FUTURE
VOTE NORTH!
VOTE BOREALIS
98-51

I drew this while I was consulting for Kluane National Park. I love scenes where Marten and Skookum interact with wildlife on an equal basis. It's just one big community out there and that's how it should feel.

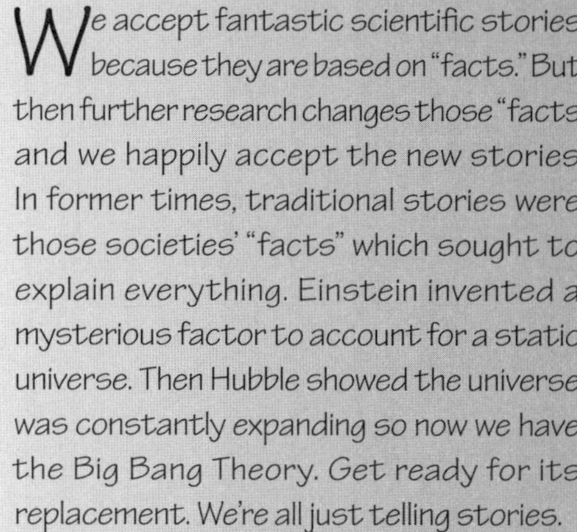

We accept fantastic scientific stories because they are based on "facts." But then further research changes those "facts" and we happily accept the new stories. In former times, traditional stories were those societies' "facts" which sought to explain everything. Einstein invented a mysterious factor to account for a static universe. Then Hubble showed the universe was constantly expanding so now we have the Big Bang Theory. Get ready for its replacement. We're all just telling stories.

The shoot 'em up era is passing in the north. You don't see nearly as many bullet holes in signs any more. Except in Alaska.

THAT'S THE $500 FOR YOUR MOTOR!
THERE'S ONLY $435 HERE?
BUT THAT'S THE $500 VIC GAVE ME FOR THE WOOD!
JILL GAVE ME THAT FOR THE DOG SLED!
AND I GOT IT FROM FRED FOR THE CHAINSAW!
GOOD GOD!! YOU MEAN NOBODY'S COUNTED IT UNTIL NOW?!!
ARE YOU SAYING NORTHERNERS ARE STUPID CHEATERS?
UM!...UM! SIMPLE? TRUSTING?
98-52
©D.URQUHART

In isolated communities, handling money can be a ritualized process akin to the rituals it arose from — the tallying and transfer of debts. Counting money you receive is a huge insult. Asking to be paid is a social faux pas. In Atlin, I had a heck of a time getting an old Frenchman to charge me for his backhoe services. He kept saying his wife would get a bill to me. Finally, I made a special trip over to his house before we both forgot what I owed.

YOUR TALK WITH WINCHESTER SURE HAD AN EFFECT!! DID YOU IMPRESS HIM WITH THE JOYS OF MUSIC? THE VALUE OF LEARNING? THE NEED FOR PRACTICE? COMMITTMENT TO A TASK?
NOPE!
I ASKED MIKE THE NEW CORPORAL TO DRIVE BY OUR PLACE EVERY TUESDAY AFTERNOON!
THEN I TOLD WINCH IT WAS THE...
ROYAL CONSERVATORY OF MUSIC POLICE!!
RCMP
98-53
©D.URQUHART

The cliché is kids are so wise. Actually, they are incredibly literal and gullible. Ten years of piano lessons for my daughter and son inspired this strip. Added to it is a subtheme, that in a small town you actually could get the local cop to do something like this.

WHAT ARE YOUR WILDERNESS RECREATION VALUES?
WELL, UM...WE POKE AROUND IN THE BUSH A LOT! PICK SOME BERRIES, CATCH A FEW GRAYLING, SHOOT GROUSE...
HMMM...THERE'S NO BOXES ON THE FORM FOR THAT! HOW'S THIS?
OTHER:
RESPONDENTS HIKE TO UNSPECIFIED DESTINATIONS ON UNCLASSIFIED TRAILS IN UNDESIGNATED PORTIONS OF UNPROTECTED CROWN LAND
DOES THAT MEAN WE'RE FAILURES?
NOPE! JUST THAT THERE'S NO BOX FOR FREEDOM!!
98-54
©D.URQUHART

I did this while consulting for the Yukon government's Protected Areas Strategy, where the strictly bureaucratic approach was missing some important wilderness values. My friend, Ben Moise, however, inserted the phrase, "poke around in the bush" into the introductory section of the strategy, based on a public comment from Mayo. It created a flurry of inter-office memos and attempts to remove it as trivializing this important document. But Ben stuck to his guns and it stayed.

1998

ANYONE SUFFERING FROM BACK PAIN? SORE LIMBS? ACHING TRUNK??!!
HERE!
HERE!
HERE!
HELP! HELP!
©D. URQUHART
98-55

THERE YA GO!!

DR. SKOOKUM Ph.D.* BUSH CHIROPRACTOR!

*PRETTY HELPFUL DOG

This is a fun thing to do in the bush and you fancy you can feel the relief as the little trees spring erect. Even though chiropractors don't have a Ph.D., which originally meant Doctor of Philosophy, I added it as a joke because everybody is a doctor these days. The exalted status this term used to carry was jokingly called "Ph deification."

HOLY COW! GIANT MOOSE TRACKS!!
98-44
COULD BE CARIBOU?

TOO POINTED! NO DEWCLAW PRINTS!
CAN'T BE GOAT OR SHEEP?!!

AND WHAT ELSE HAS A CLOVEN HOOF?!!
DUNNO! DOESN'T THAT BEAT THE DEVIL?!!

NOT QUITE GENTLEMEN!
©D. URQUHART

This strip covers a couple of themes. First, northerners love to analyse tracks. And second, it is often difficult to tell moose from caribou tracks, especially in winter. I wonder if this strip prompted any letters to the editor due to religious sensitivities.

Officialdom

1999

THE PROBLEM DOMAIN IS THE FUNCTIONAL SOCIAL SYSTEM WHICH IS CONCEPTUALIZED BY PROCESSES THAT...
OH! I SEE! SO I JUST SIT BACK AND SOMEHOW THROUGH THE MYSTERIOUS CHANNELS OF YOUR TIGHT LITTLE BUSH COMMUNITY MAGIC WILL HAPPEN!!
98-19
YEP IT WILL!

Unlike southerners who seldom interact with elected officials or bureaucrats, northerners are constantly confronted with all levels of government representation and administration. Within the community, complications arise where residents often see each other in many different roles and relationships. As well, there is a constant influx of bureaucrats from "headquarters" with bizarre projects and outrageous notions about the north.

AS CHAIRMAN OF THE WILDLIFE COUNCIL I SAY NO ROAD IN THIS VALLEY!
95-9
BUT AS CHAIR OF THE BOARD OF TRADE I SAY YES!
©D.URQUHART

HOW COME WOOD BURNS?
©D. URQUHART
WELL, TREES TAKE ENERGY FROM THE SUN AND CARBON FROM THE AIR!

TO MAKE WOOD AND WHEN IT BURNS...

THE ENERGY IS RELEASED AS HEAT AND THE CARBON GOES BACK IN TO THE AIR!
99-1

SO FIRE IS REALLY **RECYCLED SUNSHINE!**
AND TREES ARE EARTH'S BATTERIES!

To be able to stop almost anywhere in the bush, pick up some "lifeless" sticks from the ground and create light and warmth from them is truly a miracle – perhaps the first miracle we ever recognized. A British scientist, James Jeans, wrote, "Life exists in the universe only because the carbon atom possesses certain exceptional properties." Northern coniferous forests are now prized as a vital carbon "sink" in the lifegiving (and polluting) carbon cycle.

SPYING THE TINY HOLE IN THE SNOW, THE ARCTIC WOLF POUNCES ON ITS TINY PREY!!
©D. URQUHART

DISPATCHING IT INSTANTLY WITH A VIOLENT SHAKE OF THE HEAD!
99-2

ANOTHER PIECE OF HOT DOG SKOOK?!!

DON'T LAUGH! IT COULD COME IN HANDY SOME DAY!!

Huskies are a delightful combination of "primitive" carnivore and house pet. We call our dog "Cisco" a "housky" because he is our first sled dog that's lived inside with us.

FIRST HE MADE US GO THROUGH OVERFLOW! THEN FLUFFY SNOW! THEN MORE OVERFLOW! AND MORE FLUFFY SNOW!!

©D. URQUHART

WELL, THAT WOULD EXPLAIN IT!!
99-3

Though they have evolved in the north, sled dogs have a lot of foot problems. Sometimes I dipped their feet into pine tar to toughen them and they would leave a trail of brown footprints for a half mile in the snow. Often, when you stop for a rest, your team will immediately collapse and set about chewing snowballs out of their feet.

CAREFUL MARTEN!

DON'T WORRY SKOOK! ONLY US VETERAN NORTHERNERS ARE SAFE HERE!

99-4

WE DON'T BELONG IN THE NEW MILLENIUM!
©D.URQUHART

This was prompted by an extreme sport competition televised from Valdez, Alaska. A bunch of "Hey! Dude!" California kids traversing perpendicular glaciers, leaping off cliffs and outrunning their own avalanches, having a once in a lifetime narrow escape on every run, only to stop at the bottom, belt back a beer and say, "Cool!" Where does that leave the intrepid bushman?

BETTER CHECK OL' JAKE! IF HE RUNS OUT OF FIREWOOD HE STARTS TO BURN THE FURNITURE AND EVEN SOME PARTITIONS!!

BUT HE LOOKS OKAY THIS TIME!!
HEY! MARTEN! YOU ARRIVED...
©D.URQUHART

JUST IN TIME!!
99-5

I have heard about disadvantaged people doing this in the past and I came pretty close myself a few years ago when the temperature dipped below −40° and nobody could go out to cut or deliver firewood. Each day I was in the yard probing under the snow for old fencing, lumber scraps, anything I could find to keep the fire going. I swore never to let the wood supply sink that low again.

DAD? WHY DO SOUTHERNERS BUILD FANCY HOUSES IN FORT DOGGEREL?
BECAUSE TO GET THAT RICH THEY WRECK THEIR OWN ENVIRONMENT!!

99-6
SO THEY HAVE TO FIND A PLACE WHERE THAT HASN'T HAPPENED!
ARE YOU GOING TO GET RICH BY WRECKING THE NORTH?

HEY! I MIGHT BE POOR IN THE POCKET BOOK BUT I'M ALREADY RICH IN THIS LAND AND MY FREEDOM TO ENJOY IT!
AND WE'VE BECOME A CARETAKER COMMUNITY! THEY PAY FOR THE BIG HOUSES AND WE BUILD AND TAKE CARE OF THEM!

Many northern towns,especially outside larger centres, have a housing double standard with stylish modern homes belonging to southerners, Europeans or retirees, and smaller, modest places for locals. You can also tell the local places by the accumulation of equipment outside which is where such people really live.

THE MID WINTER TRIP TO THE BIG SMOKE! IT'S NOT THE SHOPPING OR THE FOOD OR THE SHOWS!
FOR A BUSH FAMILY...
IT'S THE HOTEL ROOM!!
© D. URQUHART
99-7

Imagine coming from a small log cabin with propane lights and maybe a propane fridge or a plywood box outside for frozen food. You heat water on the wood cookstove and there's a water barrel in the corner with a dipper on a nail above it. Under the sink, if you have one, is a "slop pail" that must be emptied regularly. Your radio is battery operated.

WHY DO HUMANS HAVE SUCH LITTLE NOSES AND EARS?
EVOLUTION! LONG AGO THEY LOOKED NORMAL!
99-8

BUT AS THE CLIMATE COOLED, THEIR EXPOSED PARTS KEPT FREEZING OFF!
© D. URQUHART

AND NOWADAYS ITS SO BAD THE YOUNG ONES...

HAVE TO KEEP THE PIECES PINNED TOGETHER WITH BITS OF METAL!!

I have had several requests to reprint this one. When you think of it, except for cats (lynx, cougars), most northern mammals have long furry faces and big ears. We must look pretty weird to them.

VEE ARE DISAPPOINTED YOU FAMOUS NORTH VOODSMAN IS HAFING T.V. IN LOG CABIN!
99-9
BUT I STAY OUT HERE FOR MONTHS AT A TIME AND...

BESIDES I...
SHHHH!

SCHEISST! SCHEISST!
GO! GO! GO!!!
WORLD CUP HOCKEY!
© D. URQUHART

"Scheisst!" is German for "Shoot!" People who come to the north for a "wilderness" experience are not looking for the same thing as a northerner who "lives" in or near the bush. When we lived full-time in the bush, we were glued to our AM radio. Radio news and documentaries actually enhanced the contrast between "modern" hectic society and our simple lives where we only saw other people a couple of times a year.

LOVIN' FLIRTIN'
CHEATIN' HURTIN'
LYIN' LOOSIN'

SIGHIN' BOOZIN'
CRYIN' DENYIN'
DYIN' LEAVIN'
GRIEVIN'

99-10
GREAT C&W MUSIC, EH?!!
THIEVIN' DISBELIEVIN'

@#* SOUTHERNERS! CAN'T EVEN APPRECIATE THEIR TRADITIONAL MUSIC!
© D. URQUHART

Country and western is the theme music of the north. It was the daily fare when I frequented Inuvik where the favourite program was called something like the "Lovin', Hurtin', Gamblin', Drinkin', Truck Drivin' and Mom Show'. The station once experimented with a classical hour but received such outrage it was soon cancelled. Cartooning is the only art medium (discounting advertising) where you use words and drawings together. Even the words can be "drawn" for effect.

YIPPEE!! I LOVE LOGGING! THEY LEAVE THE TOPS WITH CONES RIGHT ON THE GROUND JUST FOR ME!!
© D. URQUHART

YES! BUT WITH MODERN ECO-SYSTEM BASED METHODS, LOGGING MUST SIMULATE NATURAL PROCESSES LIKE FOREST FIRES...
99-11

MARSHMALLOW?

This was inspired by my consultant work with the Yukon Forest Strategy. In the past few years there has been a shift away from "species" management to "ecosystem-based" management. When I went to college, your ambition would be to be a caribou or wolf or bear biologist. Nowadays you'd look to be a "conservation" biologist or an environmental planner.

SEE? I TOLD YOU NORTHERNERS ALL GO TO HEAVEN!
© D. URQUHART

99-12
BUT WE SPENT A LIFETIME NOT RECYCLING, DUMPING GARBAGE IN THE BUSH, THROWING STUFF OUT OF CAR WINDOWS...
RELAX! WHO KNOWS ABOUT GARBAGE UP HERE?!!

THAT'S THEM!

If only...

I NEED THREE NEW CABINS FOR THE TRAPLINE!
GOT JUST THE GUY FOR YOU!
JA! VEE MAKE FOR $15000!
99-13
GEE... I DUNNO!!
OKAY! FOR $20,000!!
I.. WHAT? HEY!... AM I MISSING SOMETHING?
THEY CAN'T CUT TREES IN THEIR COUNTRY...
HE PAYS YOU!!!
ISS GOOT?!
©D.URQUHART

I have heard about such arrangements while working in several communities but can't determine whether it's true or just bar talk.

WHY'S EVERYONE STANDING HERE?
THE 'NO WALK' SIGN IS ON!
BUT THERE'S NO TRAFFIC?!

THIS IS NUTS!
©D.URQUHART

HE WALKED!
AGAINST THE SIGN!
HOW DO YOU EXPLAIN IT?
NORTHERNER!
99-14

This is silly but people love this strip. It's the kind of thing everyone relates to but would never think really worth commenting on. Jim Davis' most popular Garfield strip is where the cat is lying on his tummy just saying, "I feel down..down..down. . .dobby dooby down down. . ." He was advised not to send it in but the response when it was published was overwhelming.

HOW COME TEACHER SAYS 'EQUINOX' IS THE FIRST DAY OF SPRING?
WELL! UM... IT'S A STORY...

..UM... ABOUT A NORTHERN WARRIOR NAMED 'EQUI' WHO FINDS THE DOOR TO SPRINGTIME AND KNOCKS ON IT!
THEN WHAT ABOUT 'VERNAL'

WELL... UH... VERN AND.. AL ARE EQUI'S FRIENDS WHO... WHO...
99-15
ARE TRAPPED BEHIND THE DOOR!

GEE! THANKS GUYS! YOU SURE KNOW A LOT!!
WE'RE A TEAM!!
©D.URQUHART

For years when walking my kids to school in the spring and fall, we would comment on the changes in day light and why this was occurring. It took me some time to get the words vernal, equinox and solstice fixed in their little brains. Using Latin and Greek for all our terms sure makes things awkward.

99-16
HOW COME WOLVES AND DOGS EAT GRASS AND THROW UP EVERY SPRING?
THEY USED TO BE HERBIVORES LIKE US AND THEY MISS IT!

YOU MEAN THEY WANT TO BE LIKE US?!!
WE CALL IT 'MOOSE MIMICRY' RESULTING FROM SEVERE UNGULATE ENVY!!

AND WE CALL THAT 'MOOSOMORPHIZING' DEFINING OTHER SPECIES IN TERMS OF YOURSELF!!
OF COURSE WE HUMANS NEVER DO THAT!

"Anthropomorphizing" refers to our tendency to interpret other animals' actions as if they had human motivations. Walt Disney Studios were experts at this but scientists can easily lapse into this as well.

WELL SEE YOU GUYS!! I GOTTA CHECK MY TRAPLINE!!
99-17

HOW IMPRESSIVE! AFTER SUCH A LONG RIDE HE IS SO DEDICATED TO HIS TRAPPING VOCATION!

YESSIR! THAT ERNIE WOULD TRAP ALL NIGHT IF HE COULD!!

THEN WHAT'S SO FUNNY?

The other day at a meeting, a friend told us his 20-year-old son had gone back east to "check his trapline." We all knew what he meant.

OUR SCIENTISTS HAVE FOUND THERE ARE TWO TYPES OF MOOSE OR 'MORPHS' IN THE POPULATION!
© D. URQUHART

ONE 'MORPH' IS ENERGETIC AND ADVENTUROUS WITH LONG SEASONAL MOVEMENTS!
WHILE THE OTHER MORPH DOES LITTLE AND JUST HANGS AROUND ITS TINY HOME RANGE!
99-18

DO YOU UNDERSTAND THE CONCEPT?
OH! I THINK WE DO!!

I heard this from a biologist. Actually, there is also a population of "migratory moose" that travel over a hundred miles from northeastern Alaska to Old Crow Flats in the Yukon in order to calve in ideal habitat.

FEWER HUMMINGBIRDS THIS SPRING!!
LOGGING!
EVEN ASPENS ARE BEING LOGGED NOWADAYS!
©D.URQUHART

99-19
NOT FOR LACK OF FLOWERS!
WOODPECKERS!
WOODPECKERS MAKE HOLES IN ASPENS!

ARE SCIENTISTS AWARE OF THIS?
SAP!
IN EARLY SPRING HUMMINGBIRDS RELY ON SAP FROM WOODPECKER HOLES!

MARTEN! I NEED AN EXPLANATION!
HEY! I JUST TOLD YOU!!
TRADITIONAL KNOWLEDGE! IT'S NOT THE WORDS... IT'S HOW YOU HEAR THEM!

"TO REDUCE PRESSURE ON THE TOWN DUMP, RESIDENTS ARE ASKED TO RECYCLE AS MUCH AS POSSIBLE..."
©D.URQUHART
99-20

"DUE TO GROWING BEAR PROBLEMS IN THE COMMUNITY RESIDENTS ARE REQUESTED NOT TO LEAVE ANY ORGANIC MATERIAL OUTSIDE THEIR HOMES..."

YOU'RE MAILING OUR GARBAGE TO THE GOVERNMENT?
LET'S JUST CALL IT THE COM-POSTAL SERVICE!!

99-21
YOU WASHING FOR TWO MEN?
NO! WHY?

DEFINITELY TWO SIZES OF JEANS THERE!!

OH! THESE ARE MARTEN'S BUSH PANTS! FOR HUNTING FISHING TRAPPING LOGGING! BUT LATELY HE'S BEEN...
WHICH EXPLAINS HOW OUR MODERN LIFESTYLES ARE EXPANDING THE

WEARING THESE TOWN PANTS FOR MEETINGS RESTAURANTS AND BARS!!
ARCTIC WAISTLAND!
©D.URQUHART

This is an example of how apparently disconnected events can conspire in an ecosystem to produce unexpected impacts. Complex relationships are the kind of thing traditional knowledge deals with because it is a holistic approach to understanding the environment. Science is trending this way with ecosystem-based management and conservation biology but most decisions are still based on just cutting trees or just shooting moose.

I created this strip during a period when Whitehorse was experiencing serious bear problems. Every day, choppers would fly low over our house looking for bears. A bear broke into a neighbour's shed where some moose meat was hanging and there were radio warnings about leaving "garbage" outside. Meanwhile, other radio ads were encouraging recycling and composting.

I actually heard someone make a comment the other day about "go-to-meeting pants." The paradox is that people who are prized for their bush knowledge are also at risk of losing their bush skills and outdoor stamina because they are always in demand for meetings and presentations about bush issues.

WE'RE STOCK-PILING BOTTLED WATER AND FREEZE DRIED FOOD FOR THE MILLENNIUM MELTDOWN! HOW ABOUT YOU?!!
NO FEAR!

I CAN USE A FRIEND'S CABIN UP NORTH! PLENTY OF FRESH WATER, FISH AND GAME THERE!
WELL I GOTTA HAND IT TO YOU HAL!!
©D.URQUHART

HANGING OUT WITH THOSE NORTHERN BUMPKINS FINALLY PAID OFF!
A CYNIC KNOWS THE PRICE OF EVERYTHING AND THE VALUE OF NOTHING!!
99-22

All the millennium hype about Y2K. How is this going to look in the history of our time that we were totally obsessed with a computer bug? As I write this after the millennium, I can tell you it came in with a whimper and sadly empty celebrations. My wife and I built a fire in the bush at –35°, cooked hot dogs and drank ice cold champagne. Skookum's thought bubble is a quote from Oscar Wilde.

MY COUSIN ART'S VERY SENSITIVE SO TRY AND SAY SOMETHING NICE ABOUT HIS WORK!

IT'S A WORK OF ART!!
ART DREW IT!

DEFINITELY INTENSE!
99-23
CANVAS TENTS THAT IS!

VERY DERIVATIVE!
DERIVED FROM FINGER PAINTING!
THAT WAS WONDERFUL!
AND HE NEVER LIED!!
©D.URQUHART

This began with a daydream, while doing dishes, about the word "artwork." Art-work. . .work-of-art and that's all it takes for a cartoonist with nothing particular on his mind. "Derivative" is an in-joke used to satirize yuppies trying to act like art critics. Woody Allen also uses it.

MY CANCER PROJECT GOT A FIRST AT THE SCIENCE FAIR!
COOL!
WELL, IT LOOKS LIKE..

AND MY 'DON'T TRASH THE PLANET' POSTER IS GOING TO THE DISTRICT COMPETITION!
99-24
RIGHT ON!
THE HUMANS ARE DOING...

I GOT A B+ ON MY NORTHERN ECOLOGY EXAM!
GREAT! HEY LET'S SET FIRE TO THE MEADOW AND SMOKE OUT GOPHERS!!
A GOOD JOB OF RAISING...

... THE NEXT GENERATION OF HYPOCRITES!
©D.URQUHART

Every morning I used to walk my kids to school past trails of garbage, juice containers, potato chip bags, styrofoam noodle cups, cigarette packages, snuff cans, etc. Inside the school are science projects, displays and posters, all decrying pollution and extolling recycling. What is going on here?

AH! BACK IN THE NORTH! IT'S SO QUIET AND PEACEFUL UP HERE!!
YEP! IN FACT SOME PEOPLE USE THE NORTH AS A RETREAT FROM SOUTHERN PRESSURES!!
© D. URQUHART
99-25
WHICH REMINDS ME YOU HAVEN'T MET OUR NEW VILLAGE COUNCIL INTERN...
COUNCIL OFFICE
MONICA!
LEW!...LEW! ...LEW!!!

It's true that the north can be a haven from southern stresses and a handy escape route either from the public or the law. A surprising number of American felons are picked up on the Canadian stretch of the Alaska Highway heading to Alaska.

UH-OH! WATCH THIS STUPID DOG TURN IN TO THE ROAD!
99-26
STUPID DRIVERS!
YOU HAVE TO WATCH OUT FOR EVERY ONE!
© D. URQUHART
YEOWW!!
YIKES!!
SEE WHAT I MEAN?!
SEE WHAT I MEAN?!

This is the kind of cartoon that puzzles southerners because they rarely see dogs going about their daily business on main roads. But anyone from a northern community will instantly recognize this.

I WON'T!! I WON'T!! NO WAY!!
THERE! SEE?!!
© D. URQUHART
YOU HAVE NO WILLPOWER!!
99-27

What's even more curious is our human delight in stimulating this canine reflex.

WELL! 250 YEARS ON THIS EARTH! THINK I'LL CASH IN SOON! I'M EXHAUSTED!!
WHAT FROM? ALL YOU DO IS STAND THERE!!

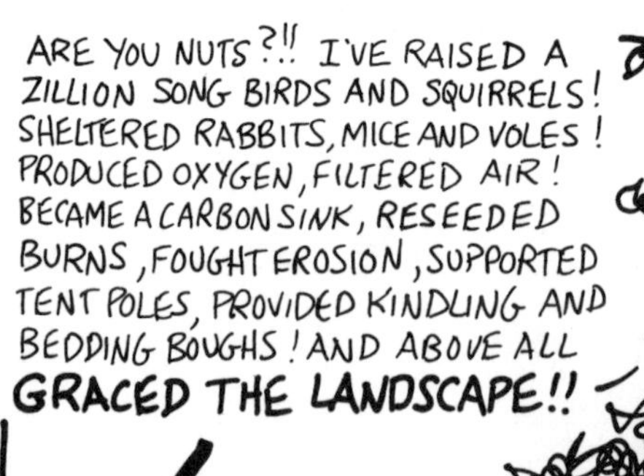
ARE YOU NUTS?!! I'VE RAISED A ZILLION SONG BIRDS AND SQUIRRELS! SHELTERED RABBITS, MICE AND VOLES! PRODUCED OXYGEN, FILTERED AIR! BECAME A CARBON SINK, RESEEDED BURNS, FOUGHT EROSION, SUPPORTED TENT POLES, PROVIDED KINDLING AND BEDDING BOUGHS! AND ABOVE ALL GRACED THE LANDSCAPE!!

99-28
THOSE ALSO SERVE WHO ONLY STAND...

When I draw spruce trees, my pen never leaves the page. The straggly scraggly spruce is the signature of the north – the "boreal forest" as scientists call it. The last outposts of the northern treeline. The dark cladding of our mountains. The humble decorations of our swamps. Pines are relative newcomers. They haven't even made it to Alaska yet.

99-29
THIS IS THE FRIGGIN' COLDEST SPRING ON RECORD! SO MUCH FOR GLOBAL WARMING!!

WELL, THE MODEL PREDICTS TEMPERATURE EXTREMES, DROUGHTS, FIRES, MONSOONS FLOODS...
THAT'S BULL! YOU HATCHED A THEORY THAT ACCEPTS EVERYTHING–AND CAN'T BE DISPROVEN!

YES! ISN'T IT WONDERFUL!!
©D.URQUHART

We must, as a society, worry. All human societies worry. Religious societies worry about obeying their God and if disasters like drought, crop failure, fire in the sky, locust plagues, etc. occur, it's because they screwed up. Technological societies worry about the same things (pollution, global warming, increased forest fires, more floods, etc.) and also blame their own actions. We will never be free from worry. It's just what we do.

WHAT'S WITH THEM?
OH! JUST MALES AND THEIR SILLY...

...LOVE OF FREEDOM AND ADVENTURE! WHEN THEY DON'T HAVE ENOUGH THEY GET DEPRESSED!!
IS THERE A NAME FOR THIS?
99-30

YEP! PMS!
©D.URQUHART

POST MUSHING SYNDROME!

The Inuit word for "summer" is the "time of inferior sledding." Most of my strips are observations on northern life. But you have to create a twist to make the strip amusing.

SO? HOW WAS FORESTRY CLASS?
GREAT! A TRAPPER TOOK US OUT! WE MADE A FIRE HAD TEA AND LOOKED AT THE TREES!!

AND WHAT WAS THE LESSON?
HE CALLS IT TREE APPRECIATION!

99-31
TREE APPRECIATION?!! WHAT KIND OF MICKEY MOUSE COURSE IS THAT! WHERE'S THE SILVICULTURE? DENDROCHRONOLOGY?!! TIMBER SUPPLY ANALYSES? WE'RE ALL DOOMED!!!
THE TRAPPER AGREES! BUT HE SAYS THERE'S STILL HOPE!!
©D.URQUHART

I spent an intense couple of years consulting for the Yukon Forest Strategy – an exercise which produced many camps: industrial loggers, "Ma and Pa" operations, scientists, tree huggers, and just plain old bush rats who have no particular axe to grind but are nervous about all the rhetoric flying around.

BUSH MEN USE GAS FOR FIRES AND LIGHT THEIR MATCH ON THEIR PANTS FLY...
©D.URQUHART

LIKE THIS! SEE?!!
99-32
WHUMP!
WHICH IS WHERE YOU SPILLED THE GAS, RIGHT?

The frightening part is when you've thrown the gas on the fire, especially on a warm day, and you can't get the match lit! You strike it too hard and it breaks! Frantically you fumble for another while the fumes become stronger in your nose! By the time you toss one onto the sticks the flames sometimes blow right past your knees!

AND THERE'S A BETTER TRAIL OVER HERE!
99-33

YOU WERE VERY HELPFUL TO THOSE PRETTY YOUNG WOMEN!
WELL! WE HAVE TO BE NICE TO TOURISTS!!

AND THIS FACE OF MUSH MOUNTAIN HAS NEVER BEEN CLIMBED!
©D.URQUHART

The Yukon government initiated a "Be Nice to Tourists" campaign several years ago and even offered public courses on how to be courteous and master basic Japanese and German phrases. It was felt that our basic gruff northern manners needed polishing. The most successful program here has been the campground host program in which locals visit tourists and chat about the north.

THE TOURIST
8th day on the river....
ICE CREAM & FRENCH FRIES... huh!
ICE CREAM & FRENCH FRIES... huh!
ICE CREAM & FRENCH FRIES... huh!
©D. URQUHART
1999
ICE CREAM
FRENCH FRIES
HOT DOGS
MENU
99-34
2 hours later....
PEACE & BEAUTY... huh!
PEACE & BEAUTY... huh!
PEACE & BEAUTY... huh!
huh!... huh!... HUH!

Southerners who vacation in the bush may experience an unsettling sequence of revelations. First nervousness, then relaxation, then yearning for civilization, then culture shock when they reach town. I went through this every summer I worked up north as a student and, like some, vowed to come back and live in the bush.

YOU LIE HERE! AND YOU GET ON HER BACK!!

99-35
WHAT ARE YOU DOING?
© D. URQUHART

THINKING OUT OF THE BOX!!
COLA

While operating a weather station on the Yukon/NWT border we received a surprise litter of pups from our dog team. One puppy, who we named "Panda," was the smartest little guy I have ever seen. He was up and out of his box while the others were still staggering around with half closed eyes. I wish we could have kept him.

STEADY NOW! HOLD IT! HOLD IT! DON'T MOVE!
MAKING HIM DO TRICKS IS SILLY!
99-36

THAT'S A BOY! GOOD BOY!!
DON'T YOU THINK ITS DEMEANING?

NO! HE LIKES TO LEARN AND IT MAKES HIM FEEL IMPORTANT!
© D. URQUHART

JUST A SECOND MORE! GOOD BOY! GOOD BOY!

This wouldn't work for other strips because the animals don't speak directly to the people. Snoopy can wear a fighter pilot hat, Garfield can pour coffee – but they can't talk. Communicating with an animal seems far less of a stretch to me but nobody does it except for Dilbert where the animals have professional careers. But weirdest of all is Walt Disney, with a mouse as big as a dog and "humans" with black noses and droopy ears.

99-37
HEY MARTEN! GOT BUSTED AND DOIN COMMUNITY SERVICE?
NOPE! VOLUNTEER!
IT'S A PRIVILEGE TO HAVE TIME AND FREEDOM TO CARE FOR THE LAND!!
OR MAYBE YOU'D RATHER HAVE YOUR BUTTS SHOT OFF LIKE IN KOSOVO!
AND PICKING LITTER SAVES US FROM THAT?
WELL! CARING FOR THE LAND AND FOR PEOPLE IS ALL CONNECTED SOMEHOW!!
AND YOU THINK WAR IS A SMART IDEA?!!
THIS IS A DUMB IDEA!!

What a contrast to watch the Bosnian war on television and then step outside to a free world that we take way too much for granted. Most Kosovars would die for the peace and freedom to just clean up around their community. In fact they are.

DEAR PROFESSOR SKOOKUM:
"Do huskies have a conscience? Do they feel any guilt?
99-38
"WHENEVER I AM TORN BETWEEN TWO EVILS, I CHOOSE...
©D. URQUHART
THE ONE I NEVER TRIED BEFORE!!

This is a quote from Mae West – a 1930s film star who loved to shock people with her naughtiness. In her own words, "I used to be Snow White…but I drifted."

SO! WE'RE ALL GOING TO THE JOB INTERVIEW TOMORROW?
YEAH! BUT I AIN'T DRESSIN' UP OR NUTHIN'
I'M JUST GONNA BE ME! TAKE IT OR LEAVE IT!
AND I SURE AIN'T KISSIN THEIR BUTTS!
99-39

©D. URQUHART
NEXT!

This comes from a conversation with a young man wearing a mackinaw on a flight from Toronto to Vancouver. He was a sales agent for a pharmaceutical company and he took every opportunity to wear "bush clothes" because his job required him to wear a suit every day. I sketched this cartoon on the plane as we talked.

DANG! ANOTHER SNAG!!
99-40
YOU MUST BE THE STUPIDEST ANIMAL IN THE NORTH!!
COOL DAD!!
GET THE TARP!
COUGH! CHOKE! GASP!! OKAY!! SECOND STUPIDEST!!

I worked on this cartoon for years. It arose from noticing how many trees are doomed to support other deadfalls most of their lives. Then I thought about how, despite millions of years chewing wood, beavers never evolved any sense about felling trees. Then I thought about how First Nations used to store teepee poles under large spruces and it eventually came together. Snag is the logging term for a dead tree that is not lying down.

NICE SUNNY DAY!!!
ACTUALLY THERE'S NO SUCH THING AS SUNSHINE! OUR EYES TURN ELECTROMAGNETIC RADIATION INTO A SUNNY DAY IN OUR HEADS!

FOR TREES IT'S A BLACK WORLD EVERY DAY!!
IS THAT TRUE?
©D.URQUHART

99-41
NICE SHIRT!
THANKS! I THOUGHT SO!!

I read somewhere that what we see is our eyes' best guess as to what's out front. While it may be intriguing to scientifically dissect natural phenomena, it's no way to "live" on this earth. I will always think of trees as being happy or weary or uncomfortable. And besides, who cares? People think too much (my wife often accuses me of this). Emerson says, "They [the trees] nod to me and I to them." So be it.

HE IS SUCH A FOOL!! WHY DO WE HANG AROUND WITH HIM?!

GENES AND REPRODUCTION! AND RUT IS ONLY FOR A MONTH! THEN HE'S SERVED OUR PURPOSE!!!
YEAH! HOW WOULD YOU LIKE TO BE STUCK WITH HIM ALL YEAR?!!
99-42

LIKE THE POOR HUMAN FEMALES!
WHAT A SACRIFICE FOR HER SPECIES!!
D. URQUHART

I hear my wife's voice when I read the first line. She has a low tolerance for the baser male instincts – as do most women I believe. No northern mammals that I am aware of mate for life. Are their females happier?

99-43
SO? WHAT'S AN ELDER LIKE YOU THINK ABOUT 4-WHEELERS?
BETTER FOR THE ROMANCE!!

OLD DAYS IN BUSH MAN AND WOMAN WALK SINGLE FILE!

NOWADAYS WALK SIDE BY SIDE!!

This arose from my past 35 years in the bush which predates the off road vehicle era.

LET'S TAKE A W-A-L-K TO THE L-A-K-E!
SURE! SO THE D-O-G-S CAN HAVE A GOOD R-U-N!

WHAT'S UP?

99-44
WELL, THEY'RE SPELLING! SO EITHER WE'RE GOING TO THE LAKE OR...

...TO THE VET'S TO GET NEUTERED!!

Not only do animals learn certain words, they also learn intonations. Consequently, when you start spelling, your voice changes and your pet knows something is up. Famous animal behaviourist, Konrad Lorenz, had a parrot that always said goodbye to his guests – but never if they just faked leaving, no matter how cleverly they tried to do it.

99-45
OH! LOOK! A MOOSE!

MOOSE... STEAKS.. ..COOKING.. FOOD... ..STORES... SHOPPING.. ..GROCERY LIST.. EGGS ..BREAD, CREAM, SUGAR ... COFFEE!!
MOOSE... HUNTING.. ...BOOM!... SKINNING.. ..MEAT... RIBS... ..FIRE... POT... ..CUPS... COFFEE!!

STOP FOR COFFEE?
MAN! WE SURE THINK ALIKE!!

Note Rosie's hair in the first panel. Ever since she was a little girl my daughter, Kaitlyn, has filled in the blacks for these drawings. She missed this one. Actually, everyone is astonishingly unique in their thoughts and opinions as this is meant to illustrate. Someone once observed that between the closest couples there is still a chasm of 10,000 differences.

Verse
SONG OF THE NORTH
OH! THE ECONOMIC DIVERSITY AND SUSTAINABLE DEVELOPMENT TASK FORCE CAME TO TOWN!
WITH FLIPCHARTS AND DOUGNUTS AND FRIED CHICKEN FROM THE CITY!
AND 3 YEARS LATER MARTEN FOUND A STACK OF ECONOMIC DIVERSITY AND SUSTAINABLE DEVELOPMENT POSTERS IN THE REC CENTRE FURNACE ROOM!!
Chorus
99-46
And the locals watched! And the locals laughed!
And the locals chewed! And the locals laughed!
And the locals cheered! And the locals laughed!

Federal government programs, hatched in Ottawa, make almost no sense by the time they reach northern communities. In a classic manoeuvre, the bureaucrats address the lack of community interest, not by making their programs more relevant, but by bringing goodies to decoy the locals. This strip had so much text that I could not afford text boxes.

I AM A RIVER FLOWING THROUGH TIME..
CHANNELLED BY FATE CHARTED IN MIND...
BORN ON THE MOUNTAIN DEAD IN THE SEA...
THE CURRENT BETWEEN IS WHAT I CALL ME
99-47
© D. URQUHART

In his 20th anniversary Garfield edition, Jim Davis published a high school poem of his that he always wanted to use. This is mine, although I wrote it 25 years ago when my wife and I lived in the bush. It was rejected by a poetry magazine, so, like Jim, I thought, "Hell! I'll publish it myself!"

YOU KNOW THERE'S NOTHING BETWEEN THE TOP OF YOUR HEAD AND THE SUN!
AND IF GRAVITY EVER CLICKED OFF YOU'D JUST DRIFT AWAY INTO OUTER SPACE FOREVER?!!

99-48
JUST A THOUGHT!
© D. URQUHART

There are some strange anomalies in life. Can't cure the common cold. Can't figure out what gravity is. We are no further ahead than Newton, who stressed his laws described motions of bodies that behaved as if they were attracted but that only a fool would believe they actually were. Einstein didn't. He said they warped space like a bowling ball on a trampoline. Physicists are desperately seeking a unification theory that will explain all the mysterious forces of nature.

WHAT'S MILLENNIUM MEAN, ANYWAY?
I THINK IT'S THE STUFF THEY MAKE POP CANS OUT OF!
YOU MEAN THE ADULT WORLD IS MAKING ALL THIS FUSS OVER A BETTER BEVERAGE CONTAINER?!!
CELEBRATE the NEW MILLENNIUM!
FORT DOGGEREL RECREATION CENTRE
THEY MUST BE VERY SHALLOW PEOPLE!
©D. URQUHART
99-50

It took me all year to learn how to spell "Millennium" properly. I hand delivered this strip to the *Yukon News* to make sure they printed it on time.

WE CALL THAT BAY 'OPRAH'!
©D. URQUHART
BECAUSE IT'S 'WIND FREE'!
AND THAT RIDGE THERE IS 'MICK'!
BECAUSE IT'S 'JAGGED'!
AND THAT'S MADONNA MOUNTAIN!
99-51
NEVER MIND!!

Local names are always intriguing. I hate the pompous names bestowed by explorers and surveyors. An elder told me First Nations never name places after people but always in relation to a story about the location. The Yukon land claim agreement established the Yukon Geographical Place Names Board which considers new names or revisions. The sooner they get rid of British royalty and Canadian Governors General, the better.

A SUDDEN COLD SNAP AND WE'RE ALL STANDING OUT ON THE LAKE?
SH-H-H! HERE IT COMES!!
RUM! RUM!
ZAK! ZAK!!
ZAK! ZAK!
AK! AK!
©D. URQUHART
WOW! HAL! RIGHT BETWEEN YOUR LEGS!!
I PEED MY PANTS!!
99-52

When we lived in the bush we would lie in bed and listen to the lake booming and moaning all night during cold snaps in the late fall. During the day, while checking fish nets or travelling on the lake, occasionally a distant rumble would thunder towards us as a crack spread. Even though you know it's safe, it is a frightening experience.

OKAY! BUSHMAN! WHAT MADE THIS TRACK?
GEE! IT'S SO DEEP! BUT SO NARROW?!! I GIVE UP!!
99-53
WOULD YOU BELIEVE A DASCHUND WITH A BIG TAIL?
TOUGH SLOGGING EH, FRED?!!
©D.URQUHART

Animal tracks are a wonderful source of information and speculation. I tried to think of something that would puzzle even an expert.

WELL, I DON'T KNOW WHAT THEY SAID ABOUT TRAPLINE TOURS BUT...
..THIRTY BELOW AND BLOWING SNOW IS COMMON IN DECEMBER!
©D.URQUHART
SO! YOU MAKE AN EFFIGY FROM PINE CONES! NAME IT AFTER YOUR TRAVEL AGENT AND THROW IT IN THE FIRE!
THIS IS STRANGELY SATISFYING!!
99-55

Trapline tours are relatively new to the north and a clever diversification of the meager options facing anyone who wants to make a living from the bush. Notice Marten's mitts hanging on "idiot strings" – also the Billy stick and the fire sunk into the snow.

ZEE GERMAN NETWORKS WON'T BUY ZISS ARCTIC HEROES FILM!!
©D.URQUHART

YESTERDAY ZAY PLAY HOCKEY MIT CANOE PADDLES UNT FROZEN DOG POOP!!

NOW ZAY ARE CATCHING SNOW FLAKES MIT ZEE TONGUE!!
99-56

ZAY ARE NOT MIGHTY TRAPPERS ZAY ARE DUMPKOFF NINCOMPOOPS!
WISE FOOLS ARE THEY WHO PLAY AT WORK AND WORK AT PLAY!

The German fascination with the Canadian north is intriguing. German kids are raised on arctic adventure stories. There are always German films being made in the Yukon and I suspect they tend to focus on very cliché images. Ironically, living in the bush tends to bring out the kid in you – not the hero. Skookum's bubble is my own and not a quotation that I know of. But I read so many it is hard to tell.

@☆* TOWN COUNCIL! STUPID GOVERNMENT! SILLY SCHOOL BOARD! CRAZY DOCTOR! FRIGGIN' MORTGAGE! CAR PAYMENTS! MEAN TEACHERS, KIDS CLOTHING...
...POOR FUR PRICES! NEW TRAPLINE! NEW CABIN! NICE LAKE! PRETTY...
MOUNTAINS! GREAT SLEDDING! BEAUTIFUL DAY!!! FREEDOM!!
BUSH THERAPY!
©D. URQUHART
99-57

I spent some time composing this. I see I forgot the trailing thought bubbles in the one nearest Marten. You can see how making Skookum black increases your focal attention on him even though he is very small.

Science

My own scientific background has made me particularly hard on scientists, however, they've taken my satires with great tolerance. Classical science based on academic principles is both appreciated and despised by northerners who, until recently, have often been egregiously ignored and patronized by "experts" from the south.

I'M A COMPUTER ANALYST BUT I ALWAYS WANTED TO BE A WILDLIFE BIOLOGIST
96-39

THERE ARE NO MOOSE THERE!
OH YES! WE HAVE A GIS PROGRAM
LIES, DAMNED LIES AND STATISTICS!

YOU'RE LUCKY TO OBSERVE REAL WILDERNESS SCIENCE IN ACTION!!

JANUARY 1, 2000! BIGGEST HANGOVER OF THE CENTURY!
00-01
©D.URQUHART

KNOW HOW YOU CAN TELL?

EVERYONE FORGOT THEIR PLUG-INS!!

BOY! I THOUGHT CALIFORNIA WAS MODERN BUT YOU GOT MORE ELECTRIC CARS THAN THEM!
THOSE ARE PLUG-INS FOR PAN HEATERS, BLOCK HEATERS AND BATTERY BLANKETS!!
©D.URQUHART

OTHERWISE THE OIL WILL BE LIKE PEANUT BUTTER, THE COOLANT WILL BE LIKE A LIME SLUSHY AND THE BATTERY WOULDN'T RUN A WALKMAN!!

HEY! WHERE YOU GOING?
CANCEL MY INTERNET ORDER FOR AN ELECTRIC CAR FROM L.A.!!
00-02

GEE! 45 BELOW AND I SMELL WOODSMOKE EVERYWHERE! I THOUGHT IT WENT STRAIGHT UP AT THESE TEMPERATURES!!
SPONTANEOUS COMBUSTION!

©D.URQUHART

ICE CRYSTALS FOCUS SUNLIGHT ON PINES AND THEY BURST INTO FLAMES!!
YOU CAN CALL IT "FROST FIRE" AND TELL ALL YOUR SOUTHERN FRIENDS ABOUT IT!

AND WE'LL CALL IT A THERMAL INVERSION AND TELL ALL OUR FRIENDS ABOUT YOU!
00-03

A woman recently mentioned this strip to me as being very apropos of her millennium. The Yukon has the highest alcohol consumption per capita in Canada but on New Year's eve there were no drunk driving charges in Whitehorse. So what does this mean? People still drink a lot – but they plan better.

Years ago my father-in-law took me to his favourite auto store in San Diego, "Pep Boys," claiming that they stocked everything. However, they had never heard of "plug-ins" and during my explanation their expressions clearly showed they felt I was either drunk or from an institution.

Normally, in the winter, air temperature increases with altitude. Under such conditions, columns of warm, smoke-filled air naturally rise because the surrounding ground level air is denser. But sometimes a cold air mass will trap warmer air beneath it so that smoke from warm chimneys drifts around at ground level.

WE'RE A RICH COUNTRY TO OWN ALL THIS LAND RIGHT?!!
NOBODY OWNS IT! WE'RE JUST HERE TO LOOK AFTER IT AND PASS IT ON TO GOOD HANDS!
WHY US AND NOT OTHER ANIMALS?
BECAUSE WE KNOW BEST THAT THE LAND NEEDS CARE AND PROTECTION!
PROTECTION FROM WHO?
FROM US!!
©D.URQUHART
00-04

This is based on many, many conversations with First Nations people and conservationists. A rare point on which they both agree.

TWO MONTHS ON THE TRAPLINE! SO GREAT TO GET AWAY FROM THE HUSTLE AND BUSTLE!
THE HURLY BURLY!!
HOI POLLOI!
HOITY TOITY
THE HIPPITY HOPPITY RANGI DANG DOOOO!!
WE NEED TO GET BACK!!
00-05
© D.URQUHART

"Hoi Polloi" is Greek for "the many." You don't hear it any more but I remember my mother using it. Isolation from human society is very disinhibiting. It doesn't matter what you wear, what you say or what you do – nobody is watching. After 3½ years of isolation, my wife and I had a tough time readjusting to civilization.

SO? HOW WAS YOUR SKI?
DISGUSTING!! SOME KIDS PEED THEIR NAMES RIGHT BESIDE THE TRAIL!!
YOU SHOULD HAVE A SERIOUS WORD OR TWO WITH...
"MARTENIZER" AND
THE "VICTORINATOR"!!
©D.URQUHART
00-06

"Victorinator" was my daughter's suggestion because kids like to modify their names to sound like "The Terminator." Martinizer is, of course, a pun. Some people have trouble with my "toilet humour" and letters are sent to the papers but others like it. Basically, though, I think most northerners are earthy people.

ALL RIGHT! SKOOKUM! HOME IN 10 HOURS!!
00-07

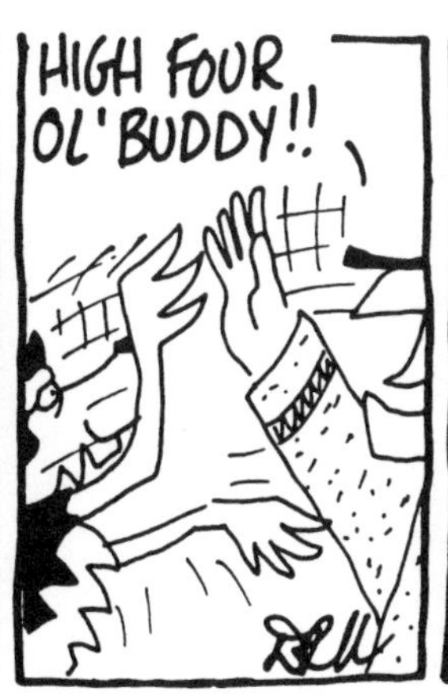
HIGH FOUR OL' BUDDY!!

TSK! TSK! YOU NORTHERN BUMPKINS! IT'S HIGH FIVE!!
© D. URQUHART

NOT WITH A SLED DOG IT AIN'T!!!

Sophistication is such a deep human trait and language is our nastiest tool in its employ. Shaw wrote, "It is impossible for an Englishman to open his mouth without making some other Englishman hate or despise him." Actually, northerners are masters at reverse sophistication in their manner of dress and speech. This often deceives southerners who become embarrassingly patronizing.

OH! MY GOD!!

OH! MY GOD!!
TAXI

OH! MY GOD!!
© D. URQUHART

SO? HOW WAS YOUR TRIP?
THERE ARE TOO MANY @A* PEOPLE IN THE WORLD!!!
© D. URQUHART
00-08

I drew this strip then went "outside" for a two-week business trip. Boy, was I right!

I'LL HELP YOU TIDY UP YOUR SHOP!!

HERE! THIS CAN GO!!
NO! THAT'S MY COLLECTION OF SMOOTH ROUND STONES!

GOOD GRIEF! HOW MANY SMOOTH ROUND STONES DOES ONE GROWN MAN NEED!!!

AM I SUPPOSED TO ANSWER THAT?
© D. URQUHART
00-09

I think most people interested in the out-of-doors are apt to collect stuff – driftwood, pine cones, dried plants, etc. It's just that northerners are more interested in the out-of-doors and are out there more so they collect more stuff – but especially rocks. You often find the odd rock in the back of a pick-up or under the seat, and shops are where most of these drift to.

WOW! 37 E-MAILS! I MUST BE IMPORTANT!!
YIKES! 52 E-MAILS! I AM EXTREMELY IMPORTANT!!
75 E-MAILS!!
GEE HAL! I THOUGHT YOU WERE A BIG SHOT? DOESN'T SOMEONE SCREEN THAT E-MAIL GARBAGE FOR YOU?
©D. URQUHART
00-10

I must hear a subtle, "I'm so important," e-mail comment every week. People did not suddenly become extra busy, it is just a c.c. button on the screen.

LOOK COOL! ACT COOL! BE COOL! ..SO COOL!!
HEY! THERE'S MARTEN
YO! MARTEN!!
DON'T DO THAT!!!
YOU'LL DRAW ATTENTION TO US!!
©D. URQUHART
00-11

Our society is a modern veneer over deeply tribal instincts and no more so than teenagers who exhibit the incredibly tense dynamic between wanting to rebel and needing to conform.

OH! NO!
WHAT'S THE MATTER?
I DRIED UP!!!
BUS
MAIL
TRASH
00-12

Every day I watch my dog eke out his supply over as many sites as he can. I like the open clean look of this strip. You can get away with so much in cartooning – like omitting the background.

ATTA HUMAN! ATTA HUMAN!! ATTA HUMAN!! GOOD HUMAN!! GOOD HUMAN!! THAT'S A GOoOOooD HUMAN!!
©D. URQUHART

NOW DOESN'T THAT SOUND RIDICULOUS?!!

I NEVER SAW IT LIKE THAT BEFORE!!
00-13

WHY ARE THEY CALLED PUPS?!
00-14

BECAUSE WHEN YOU WIND UP THEIR LITTLE TAILS THEIR LITTLE MOTORS GO...

PUP-PUP-PUP-PUP!!
AND WHEN THEIR LITTLE MOTOR'S OVERHEAT, THEY LEAK COOLANT ALL OVER THE FLOOR!
©D. URQUHART

Mark Twain said that humour consists of combining two commonplace ideas in a way no one has ever thought of before.

I loved raising sled dogs. Our problem was we never sold any puppies. We have still enjoyed quite a few over the years. Sharing a puppy's innocent joys of experience is one of the best tonics for tension that I know. This simple strip seems like a perfect way to end the book.

SO, THIS IS MY TRIBUTE TO THE NORTH! THERE ARE MANY BEAUTIFUL PLACES IN THE WORLD AND FRIENDLY PEOPLE...

BUT NONE SURPASS THE NORTH IN THE QUALITY OF ITS ENVIRONMENT AND INHABITANTS PLUS THE FREEDOM TO EXPLORE AND ENJOY IT!

Lost Moose, the Yukon Publishers

BOOKS FROM THE NORTH, ABOUT THE NORTH

EYES of the HUSKY
Skookum's Penetrating Insights into the Hearts & Minds of Northerners
NEW
Skookum's North
The "PAWS" Collection by Doug Urquhart
$7.95

A dog's-eye view of northern life. Doug Urquhart cartoons for northern weeklies and the locals love it. These comic strips are required reading for southern relatives or for anyone involved in government or resource management! Doug gets it!

Eyes of the Husky

Skookum's Penatrating Insights into the Hearts & Minds of Northerners

Annotated with Urquhart's stories about the strips. Covers 1994-2000

$14.95 • SOFTCOVER • 140 PAGES • ISBN 0-896758-03-3

Skookum's North

The PAWS collection

Covers 1983-1993

$7.95 • SOFTCOVER • 170 PAGES • ISBN 0-9694612-3-2

OUTDOOR ADVENTURE

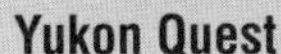

Yukon Quest

The 1,000-mile dog sled race through the Yukon and Alaska

by John Firth

Follow the teams as they travel on the ice of the Yukon River, over windswept mountains, in blizzards and bone-chilling cold.

$14.95 • SOFTCOVER • 288 PAGES • 87 B&W PHOTOS WITH MAPS • ISBN 1-896758-03-7

Wild Rivers Wild Lands
$5.95
WHITEHORSE & AREA
Hikes & Bikes
Yukon Conservation Society

Wild Rivers, Wild Lands

by Ken Madsen

Heart-stopping stories and dramatic colour photos of northern rivers and lands.

$5.95 • SOFTCOVER • 120 PAGES, OVER 75 PHOTOS, MAPS • ISBN 1-896758-01-0

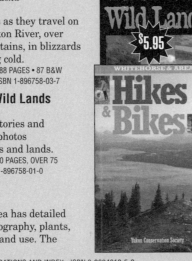

Whitehorse & Area Hikes & Bikes

by Yukon Conservation Society

This popular trail guide to the Whitehorse area has detailed maps and trail descriptions. Includes local geography, plants, wildlife, geology, weather, and First Nations land use. The essential local trail book.

$18.95 • SOFTCOVER • 160 PAGES WITH MAPS, PHOTOS, ILLUSTRATIONS AND INDEX • ISBN 0-9694612-5-9

PHOTOGRAPHY

YUKON

Yukon — Colour of the Land

photography by Richard Hartmier

A beautiful, bestselling picture book about the Yukon by a photographer who knows the land and its people. The colourful landscapes, people and places of Canada's Yukon are featured in Hartmier's first book. Witness a land renowned for its breathtaking beauty.

$18.95 SOFTCOVER, $29.95 HARDCOVER, $39.95 GIFT BOXED EDITION • 128 PAGES WITH 141 COLOUR PHOTOS • ISBN 1-896758-04-5 (SOFTCOVER), 0-9694612-7-5 (HARDCOVER)

LOST MOOSE CATALOGUES

GREAT NORTHERN
LOST MOOSE
CATALOGUE
$9.95

ORIGINAL
the lost whole moose catalogue
LOST MOOSE

Must-haves for those who love the north. These catalogues are eclectic compendium of community writing, art and photography about northern life today—part sourcebook, part almanac, part guidebook, and part storybook.

Great Northern Lost Moose Catalogue

$9.95 • SOFTCOVER • 228 PAGES • ISBN 1-896758-02-9

Another Lost Whole Moose Catalogue

$19.95 • SOFTCOVER • 156 PAGES • ISBN 0-9694612-0-8

The Original Lost Whole Moose Catalogue

$14.95 • SOFTCOVER • 112 PAGES • ISBN 0-9694612-1-6

HISTORY

Chilkoot Trail

Heritage Route to the Klondike

by David Neufeld, Parks Canada and Frank Norris, U.S. National Parks Service

This lavishly illustrated, bestselling history of this legendary trail look s past the gold rush to its origins as a Tlingit trade route, and examines First Nations use of the area today.

$24.95 • SOFTCOVER • 192 PAGES, OVER 250 B&W PHOTOS, MAPS, ILLUSTRATIONS AND INDEX • ISBN 0-9694612-9-1

EDGE OF
THE RIVER
HEART OF
THE CITY

Edge of the River, Heart of the City

A History of the Whitehorse Waterfront

by Yukon Historical & Museums Association

History of the Yukon's capital city from the gold rush through the era of the sternwheelers to the squatters today.

$12.95 • SOFTCOVER • 80 PAGES WITH B&W PHOTOS • ISBN 0-9694612-2-4

LAW OF THE YUKON
A Pictorial History of the Mounted Police in the Yukon
$9.95

Law of the Yukon

A Pictorial History of the Mounted Police in the Yukon

by Helene Dobrowolsky

Colourful history of the NWMP-RCMP over its 100 years in the Yukon, vividly told in text and pictures.

$9.95 • SOFTCOVER • 192 PAGES WITH NEARLY 300 B&W AND COLOUR PHOTOS, MAPS AND ILLUSTRATIONS, INDEX • ISBN 0-9694612-8-3

ORDER FORM ON REVERSE

ORDER FORM Please print

LOST MOOSE
THE YUKON PUBLISHERS

Name ______________________________

Address ______________________________

City ____________________ Territory/province/state ____________________

Country ____________________ Postal/zip code ____________________

☐ Payment (cheque or money order) enclosed

☐ Payment by VISA

Number ____________________

Expiry date ____________________

Signature ____________________

Title	# copies	Each	Total
Skookum's North (M)		$7.95	
Eyes of the Husky		$14.95	
Another Lost Whole Moose Catalogue (L)		$19.95	
Great Northern Lost Moose Catalogue (L)		$9.95	
Original Lost Whole Moose Catalogue (M)		$14.95	
Chilkoot Trail (L)		$24.95	
Law of the Yukon (L)		$9.95	
Edge of the River, Heart of the City (S)		$12.95	
Whitehorse & Area Hikes & Bikes (M)		$18.95	
Wild Rivers, Wild Lands (L)		$5.95	
Yukon–Colour of the Land (L) hard • soft		$29.95 • $18.95	
Yukon Quest (S)		$14.95	
		Postage & Handling	
		Subtotal	
		(Canada only) 7% GST	
		TOTAL	

Postage (surface parcel) & handling

(L)=large-size book: $4.50 within Canada, $7.50 to US, $8.50 to Int.

(M)=medium-size book: $3 within Canada, $4.50 to US, $5.50 to Int.

(S)=small-size book: $2.50 within Canada, $3.25 to US, $3.50 to Int.

Maximum $7.50 within Canada, $10.50 to US, $15.50 to Int.

Note: All prices are in Canadian dollars

Send payment to:

Lost Moose Publishing
58 Kluane Crescent
Whitehorse, Yukon, Canada • Y1A 3G7

or

Phone: (867) 668-5076, Fax: (867) 668-6223
E-mail: lmoose@yknet.yk.ca
Web site: http://www.yukonweb.com/business/lost_moose